# LOW CHOLESTEROL COOKBOOK FOR BEGINNERS

1000 Days of Delicious Low-Sodium Recipes to Manage Your Cholesterol levels and

Maintain Heart Health| with 28-Day Beginner Friendly Meal Plan to Kickstart

LINDA J. PEREZ

# Table of Contents

# Introduction

Choosing a heart-healthy, cholesterol-lowering lifestyle is a change that can benefit anyone who has high cholesterol. Inadequate exercise and eating incorrect foods are common causes of elevated cholesterol. However, a balanced lifestyle that includes exercise and eating heart-healthy foods can naturally lower cholesterol.

This low-cholesterol cookbook will explain the fundamentals of cholesterol, such as what it is and how it functions in the body. I'll review which foods are scientifically proven to lower cholesterol. And I will give guidelines to assist you getting started on your cholesterol-lowering lifestyle.

# Chapter 1
# Basics of Cholesterol

Cholesterol is a waxy component in our blood that helps the body manufacture hormones, allows certain organ functions, and helps in the digestion of vital nutrients and vitamins, including vitamin D. Cholesterol is not intrinsically "unhealthy," but too much of it can cause health concerns.

There are two sources of cholesterol. The body produces blood cholesterol in the liver, while dietary cholesterol is obtained through meals (mainly animal products like shellfish, meat, dairy, and eggs). When a doctor refers to a patient's high cholesterol, they are referring to the blood cholesterol levels that are detected during blood tests.

Although it's necessary to consume dietary cholesterol in moderation (particularly if you suffer from other health problems, such as diabetes), blood cholesterol, namely "bad" low-density lipoprotein (LDL), is the more significant health component. According to the Harvard T. C. Chan School of Public Health, the fats we eat (namely trans fats and saturated fats) influence our blood cholesterol levels more than the quantity of dietary cholesterol available in foods. Foods high in saturated fats are also high in dietary cholesterol.

Fatty meats, such as butter, palm oil, bacon, or coconut oil, processed food, and high-fat dairy, such as cheese, are examples of foods high in saturated fat that raise LDL cholesterol levels. Deep-fried meals and hydrogenated margarine are both sources of trans fats. Try to keep foods high in saturated and trans fats to rare treats as a general rule.

Olive oil, nuts like almonds and walnuts, soft non-hydrogenated margarine, and seafood like salmon are examples of unsaturated fats that support "good" high-density lipoprotein (HDL) cholesterol levels. Just keep in mind that saturated fats, like butter, are typically solid at room temperature if you are unsure if a fat is saturated or unsaturated. Vegetable oil is an example of an unsaturated lipid that tends to stay liquid.

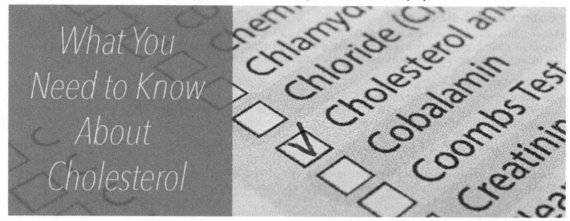

## Types of Cholesterol

Lipoproteins are two types of proteins that transport cholesterol to and from cells. LDL (low-density lipoprotein) is one of them. High-density lipoprotein, or HDL, is the other. A test determines the concentration of each type of cholesterol in your blood.

### LOW-DENSITY LIPOPROTEIN (LDL) OR BAD CHOLESTEROL

The inner walls of the arteries that provide blood to the body might gradually thicken with an excess of LDL when it circulates with the blood. It can produce plaque when combined with other chemicals (or atheroma). A thick, hard deposit known as plaque can constrict arteries, reduce their flexibility, and reduce the volume of blood they can carry. Atherosclerosis is the name given to this condition. Less blood can pass through an artery that has hardened and become narrower, leading to ischemia, or a shortage of vital nutrients. A heart attack or stroke can happen if a clot or blockage develops in a constricted artery leading to the heart or the brain.

### HIGH-DENSITY LIPOPROTEIN (HDL) OR GOOD CHOLESTEROL

HDL carries between a quarter and a third of the blood's cholesterol. Because it appears to protect against heart attacks, HDL cholesterol is classified as "good" cholesterol. Heart disease and plaque formation are both made more likely by low HDL levels (less than 40 mg/dL). To some extent, HDL "eats" up the bad cholesterol by transporting it back to the liver, where it is excreted from the body. According to some scientists, HDL helps to prevent arterial plaque from accumulating by removing extra cholesterol from the arteries.

# TYPES OF CHOLESTEROL

TRIGLYCERIDES FROM DIETARY SOURCES

INTESTINE

TG

BLOOD VESSEL

LDL LEADS TO DEPOSITION OF PLAQUE IN BLOOD VESSELS

LDL

HDL

LIVER

HDL TRANSPORTS CHOLESTEROL FROM BLOOD VESSELS TO LIVER FOR ELIMMINATION

**TRIGLYCERIDES — BLOOD FATS**

The most prevalent kind of fat in the body is triglyceride. It retains extra calories from your diet.
Fat deposits within the artery walls are associated with high triglyceride levels, high LDL (bad) cholesterol, and low HDL (good) cholesterol, which raises the risk of heart attack and stroke.

**LP(A) CHOLESTEROL**

A genetic variant of LDL (bad) cholesterol is called Lp(a). A key risk factor for the early formation of fatty deposits in arteries is a high level of Lp(a). Lp(a) is known as "bad" cholesterol, it may interact with elements in artery walls to promote the accumulation of fatty deposits.

## Normal Cholesterol Levels

In the event you need a cholesterol test, your doctor might only request a total cholesterol test. He will nonetheless request a lipogram in order to comprehend your blood cholesterol levels.

A blood test called a lipogram measures your triglyceride, cholesterol, and blood fat levels. The test findings provide you with a total cholesterol reading as well as a breakdown of your LDL and HDL cholesterol levels. Risk factors for CHD include high LDL and total cholesterol levels as well as low HDL levels.

There are fats called triglycerides in your blood as well. They retain extra or wasted calories. If you eat more calories than your body needs, the extra will be gathered as triglycerides. Raised triglyceride levels are an independent risk factor for arterial wall thickening and hardness.

## The Effect of Cholesterol on Health

Consider blood arteries to be streets and the blood that transports nutrients or oxygen to all regions of the body to be cars. Blood can reach our organs more efficiently when there is no litter or other obstacles (excellent blood flow). LDL cholesterol is like litter that steadily accumulates over time and can cause blockages that prohibit cars (our blood) from easily traveling through the streets (blood vessels). HDL cholesterol functions as a garbage truck, transporting cholesterol back to the liver to be broken down. As previously stated, diets high in saturated fats, trans fats, and unsaturated fats might increase LDL cholesterol.

When LDL cholesterol levels are excessive, plaque or blockages can form in the blood vessels, causing the arteries to constrict or harden. Heart disease, heart attacks, high blood pressure, and strokes are all increased by artery blockages and hardening. These are just a few of the reasons why we need to keep our cholesterol levels in check.

Eating less bacon and butter, limiting salt intake, and increasing fiber intake can all help decrease cholesterol and keep your heart healthy. Making these kinds of dietary modifications may appear difficult at first. When making

## CHOLESTEROL AND TRIGLYCERIDE LEVELS *in adults*

|  | TOTAL | HDL | LDL | TRIGLYCERIDES |
|---|---|---|---|---|
| **HIGH** | 240 or higher | n/a | 160 or higher | 200 or higher |
| **BORDERLINE** | 200-239 | n/a | 130-159 | 150-199 |
| **GOOD** | less than 200 | 40 or higher | less than 100 | less than 150 |
| **LOW** | n/a | less than 40 | n/a | n/a |

changes to your eating habits, it might be beneficial to begin with tiny, attainable changes and work your way up.

### RISK FACTORS

When it comes to cholesterol and heart disease, it is important to distinguish between controllable and non-controllable risk factors.

Your lifestyle decisions such as working out, eating a balanced diet, getting enough sleep, regulating your stress levels, consuming less alcohol, and quitting smoking, all fall under the category of controllable risk factors. With a few easy lifestyle adjustments, you can lower the risk factors that you can control. For instance, walk for 15 minutes three times per week for a month or prepare a delicious, wholesome supper at home rather than ordering in. When preparing those home-cooked meals, substitute fish for red meat at least twice every week.

Making a list of your present routines, such as your workout regimen, nutrition, sleep schedule, etc., and then coming up with healthier lifestyle adjustments is another strategy to improve your habits. You can jot down your thoughts in a journal and give your new objectives realistic deadlines. Celebrate your accomplishments, of course.

Non-controllable risk factors include genetics or family history, as well as age (heart disease tends to worsen as we get older) and gender (men develop incidents earlier than women). Even though you cannot change your genetic composition or your age, you can make many lifestyle adjustments to lower your cholesterol, and the recipes in this low-cholesterol cookbook will help you do just that.

## High Cholesterol Risk Factors

What should you know about your potential for high cholesterol? Although some families have a history of hyperlipidemia, there are daily decisions you can make to improve your blood cholesterol and, ultimately, your heart health.

Yes. Your way of living has a significant impact on your serum cholesterol levels. To determine if you should be concerned, go through this checklist of high cholesterol risk factors.

### 7 HIGH CHOLESTEROL RISK FACTORS

**Body weight**: You are at an elevated risk of having high cholesterol and cardiovascular heart disease if you have a body mass index (BMI) of more than 30%.

**Physical activity**: As you are probably aware, the longer you sit, the bigger your dangers. Of course, a lack of physical activity creates a variety of health problems. Exercise increases high-density lipoprotein (HDL) cholesterol, which is heart-protective, and lowers low-density lipoprotein (LDL), which is one type of blood cholesterol that increases your risk of heart disease. Even walking for 20 to 30 minutes per day can significantly lower your serum cholesterol levels and lower your risk of heart disease.

**Diet**: Food choices can either improve your blood cholesterol or cause a dangerous epidemic to form. A heart-healthy diet is abundant in dietary fiber and heart-healthy fats. Vegetables, legumes fruit, beans, and whole grains are examples of foods that provide significant dietary fiber. Equally crucial is the need to avoid, or better yet, remove highly processed meals such as baked goods, cereals, pieces of bread, pasta, and pizza crust produced with white flour, as these items induce an increase in triglycerides, another kind of blood cholesterol that is directly associated with heart disease. Saturated fats are the second type that influence your heart health risk.

Red meat, butter, and baked or prepared dishes with trans fats or lard are examples of the kinds of foods to avoid since they might cause arterial blockages. While the fact that trans fats may no longer be used in processed foods is excellent news. The University of Alabama at Birmingham's Department of Nutrition Sciences assistant professor Beth Kitchen, Ph.D., RDN, says "If you're curious about eggs and dairy products, you might be surprised to discover that new study has shown that these foods—like the fat in yogurt and the yoke of an egg—don't elevate LDL cholesterol, allowing you to continue eating them."

Since the FDA has ordered a restriction on the use of trans fats, the question becomes, what substances will the food industry employ to substitute trans fats in order to make products shelf-stable and creamy?

**Smoking**: Smoking harms your blood vessels, and harmed blood vessels are more prone to storing fatty deposits, potentially constricting the blood vessels and triggering cardiovascular problems. Furthermore, smoking is thought to reduce HDL cholesterol levels.

**High Blood Pressure:** This is related to heart health. Your blood vessels' walls can become damaged by high blood pressure, which increases the likelihood that fatty deposits will build up and cause cardiovascular issues.

**Type 2 Diabetes**: Your blood vessels become damaged when your blood glucose levels are consistently high, and as you saw with the risk factors for smoking and high blood pressure, damaged blood vessels are more prone to form plaque—the fatty deposits. Furthermore, type 2 diabetes elevates LDL cholesterol (bad cholesterol) while decreasing HDL cholesterol (the good cholesterol).

**Family History of Heart Problems**: If one of your parents or a sibling had heart disease when they were young (before age 55), you have a higher chance of getting high cholesterol, which can lead to heart disease.

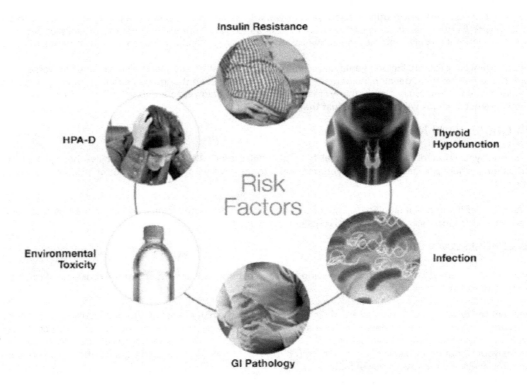

# Chapter 2
# The Management of High Cholesterol

How can high cholesterol be treated? Both medication and dietary changes are parts of the treatment. The most often prescribed medication in the world is a class of drugs called statins because high cholesterol is such a widespread health issue.

Changes in your way of life are essential to lowering your cholesterol and reducing your risk of developing more severe diseases, whether or not your doctor has recommended medication for you. You will be urged to lose weight if you are overweight. If you smoke and start working out more frequently, your doctor may also advise you to give up smoking. Aside from managing stress, having enough restful sleep is essential.

However, since saturated fat from the foods we eat is used to make cholesterol in the body, dietary adjustments will be at the top of the list of lifestyle suggestions.

## Lowering Cholesterol Through Diet

The correct tools, such as knowing the daily limits for unhealthy fats, understanding how to choose better-for-you foods, understanding how to read labels, and understanding how to prepare your kitchen, make lowering your cholesterol with a heart-healthy diet easier. Although every change is challenging at first, following these recommendations is simple after you've mastered them. I'll show you how. This book removes the guesswork from lowering your cholesterol. All the recipes are low in saturated fat, dietary cholesterol, trans fat, and sodium while high in fiber and unsaturated fats.

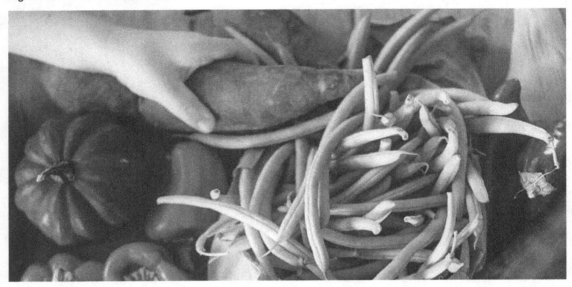

## Eating Guidelines to Lower Cholesterol

To lower cholesterol levels, the American Heart Association (AHA) suggests eating a heart-healthy diet. This involves:

Limiting saturated and trans fats: That means keeping your daily consumption of saturated fat to no more than 10% of your total calorie intake in people who are in good health. For instance, an adult consuming 2,000 calories per day with good cholesterol levels should aim for 22 grams of saturated fat or fewer. Less saturated fat—6 to 7 percent of total calories—should be consumed by people with high LDL cholesterol who are at an elevated risk for heart disease. That implies no more than 120 calories, or 13 grams, of the 2,000 calories per day that you consume should be from saturated fat.

Eating unsaturated fats: The AHA also suggests substituting unsaturated fats for saturated ones, such as butter for olive oil, and avoiding foods that contain trans fat. Unsaturated fat intake is not capped at a certain amount per day, but since all fats—even good fats—are heavy in calories, they should be consumed in moderation. The AHA provides broad recommendations for lowering cholesterol, but you should always consult a medical professional for advice specific to your needs and circumstances.

Limiting dietary cholesterol: The American Heart Association, the US Department of Agriculture, and the American College of Cardiology all urge dietary cholesterol reduction in addition to monitoring the types of fat in your diet, though exact guidelines were not offered. Fortunately, it is simple to achieve because diets low in saturated and trans fats also frequently have low levels of dietary cholesterol.

Reducing sodium: To promote heart health and decrease cholesterol, the AHA advises keeping sodium intake to 2,300 milligrams (or about 1 teaspoon of salt) each day. The salt recommendation may occasionally be much lower depending on your healthcare provider's advice and your unique needs (1,500 milligrams).

Increasing fiber: Consuming fiber is a fantastic strategy to lower cholesterol and minimize your risk of heart disease. On a daily diet of 2,000 calories, the FDA advises consuming at least 25 grams of fiber. Whole grains, legumes, vegetables, nuts, fruits, and seeds are a few foods that are good providers of dietary fiber.

Don't worry if you lack the energy to calculate the amount of fat, sodium, and fiber in each food you consume. This book will make it simple to follow these recommendations. Simply look at the nutrition bar at the bottom of each dish to see the levels of saturated and unsaturated fats, sodium, fiber, and more to help you stay on track with your health objectives.

## Choosing Foods to Lower Cholesterol

Choosing heart-healthy foods keeps the good HDL cholesterol levels up and brings down the bad LDL levels. What foods fall under this category, and how frequently should you eat them? Let's focus on some details.

Fats: Fish like tuna, salmon, and trout are excellent providers of unsaturated fats. Pick low-sodium canned fish and fresh or frozen fish options. Don't consume fried fish. Try to eat fish twice a week, either as a sandwich or wrap for lunch or as the main course at night. Other sources of unsaturated fats include nuts, seeds, soy products, and vegetable oils like olive oil. When baking or cooking, substitute olive oil for butter. Remember that coconut oil and palm oil contain more saturated fat and should be consumed in moderation. Eat nuts and seeds as a snack or as a garnish on your yogurt, oats, or homemade treats. Add tofu to soups and other foods to boost the amount of protein and good fats in your diet. Finally, since deep-fried meals like chips, French fries, donuts, and items that are battered commonly include trans fats, eating these foods in moderation is advised.

Fiber: Dietary fiber consumption usually lowers the body's LDL cholesterol levels. Vegetables, whole grains, fruits, nuts, legumes, and seeds are examples of food sources of dietary fiber. Consider increasing the amount of fresh, dried, or frozen fruit and vegetables in your daily meal. Excellent sources of fiber include whole grains like oatmeal, multigrain bread, and barley. Try to include legumes like lentils, chickpeas, and beans in soups, salads, or wraps. You can also add a small amount of nut butter to your baking. Don't forget to gradually increase your fiber intake and drink plenty of water each day to aid with digestion.

Meat and dairy: Animal products high in saturated fats include butter, full-fat dairy goods like heavy cream and cheeses, fatty types of meat, and processed meats like bologna or hot dogs. Leaner beef cuts are available at the market; substitute low-fat dairy products for these goods. Leaner cuts of meat include round, chuck, sirloin, and loin (in beef), tenderloin, and loin chop (in pork), as well as the leg, arm, and loin (in lamb). Remove and discard the skin before eating poultry.

Sodium: Lowering sodium intake can aid in lowering the risk of heart disease. Processed meats, prepared frozen foods, some canned foods, takeout food from restaurants, and takeaways frequently include high sodium levels. Be sure to read nutrition labels and avoid eating too many foods that are rich in salt.

Get rid of high cholesterol and regain control of your health with the help of this low cholesterol cookbook's amazing guidance. This Low Cholesterol Cookbook is a crucial addition to your kitchen because it will motivate you to lead a healthier lifestyle, eliminate bad fats, and enjoy the tremendous benefits of a healthier, more robust body.

Cholesterol Reducing foods

# Week 1

The meal plan for the first week of a diet low in cholesterol is included in the following. If you want to start reaping the benefits of a diet low in cholesterol, you should do your best to follow the plan to the letter.

| Meal Plan | Breakfast | Lunch | Dinner | Motivational Quotes |
|---|---|---|---|---|
| Day-1 | Vegetable Omelet | Lemon Chicken and Asparagus | Healthy Minestrone | It makes no difference how slowly you move as long as you don't stop. |
| Day-2 | Vegetable Omelet | Lemon Chicken and Asparagus | Healthy Minestrone | Don't let a mishap in the road put an end to your journey. |
| Day-3 | Breakfast Potatoes | Juicy Burgers | Pepper Steak Salad | Don't dig your own grave with your own knife and fork. |
| Day-4 | Breakfast Potatoes | Juicy Burgers | Tofu and Cucumber Spring Rolls | You feel crap when you eat crap. Continue your journey. |
| Day-5 | Couscous Cereal with Fruit | Beef Noodle Soup | Tofu and Cucumber Spring Rolls | Take things slowly at first. |
| Day-6 | French Toast | Roasted Shrimp and Veggies | Beet Walnut Salad | When you want to give up, remember why you started. |
| Day-7 | French Toast | Flank Steak with Caramelized Onions | Beet Walnut Salad | When, if not now? |

## Week 2

The following is a meal plan for the second week of a diet low in cholesterol that you can follow. The second step of the meal plan for the four weeks is the one that requires considerable consideration on your part.

| Meal Plan | Breakfast | Lunch | Dinner | Motivational Quotes |
|---|---|---|---|---|
| Day-1 | Pasta Frittata | Chicken Curry | German Potato Soup | Fall seven times, rise eight times. |
| Day-2 | Pasta Frittata | Chicken Curry | German Potato Soup | Every step, no matter how small, is a step in the right direction. |
| Day-3 | Mango Oat Smoothie | Meatloaf | Spinach Berry Salad | Taking it one pound at a time |
| Day-4 | Creamed Rice | Meatloaf | Egg White and Avocado Breakfast Wrap | You'll wish you'd started today a year from now. |
| Day-5 | Creamed Rice | Cod Satay | Grilled Vegetable Orzo Salad | With each new day comes new strength and new ideas. |
| Day-6 | Pumpkin Pie Smoothie | Tomato and Basil Quiche | Greek Pizza | Stop slacking and start making things happen. |
| Day-7 | Vegan Tropical Smoothie | Vegetarian Bolognese | Greek Pizza | The past is unchangeable, but the future is still within your grasp. |

# Week 3

The following is a meal plan for a low-cholesterol diet that should be followed for the third week. At this point, the eating plan that you followed for the prior two weeks should have begun to show results for you. Hence, in order to acquire a better outcome from the food plan, you need adhere strictly to this third stage.

| Meal Plan | Breakfast | Lunch | Dinner | Motivational Quotes |
|---|---|---|---|---|
| Day-1 | Breakfast Splits | Iron Packed Turkey | Three Bean Soup | Failure does not exist: you either win or learn. |
| Day-2 | Breakfast Splits | Iron Packed Turkey | Three Bean Soup | You can never win if you never start. |
| Day-3 | Banana Nut Smoothie | Oaxacan Tacos | Italian Eggplant Salad | You are your only constraint. |
| Day-4 | Egg Foo Young | Oaxacan Tacos | Italian Eggplant Salad | Success is not an accident: it is the result of hard work and perseverance. |
| Day-5 | Egg Foo Young | Red Snapper Scampi | Turkey Sloppy Joes | You will reap the benefits of what you plant now. |
| Day-6 | Green Smoothie with Chia and Peach | Squash and Rice Bake | Spinach, Walnut, and Black Bean Burgers | If you know you can do better, then go ahead and do it. |
| Day-7 | Celery Smoothie with Apple and Banana | Squash and Rice Bake | Spinach, Walnut, and Black Bean Burgers | Never let your fears dictate your destiny. |

# Week 4

Our meal plan for the low-cholesterol diet that we will follow for the next four weeks has reached its conclusion. At this point, you have already ingrained the behavior of consuming a diet low in cholesterol into your routine. Therefore, make sure you go through this final stage to receive the finest possible results for both your body and your mind.

| Meal Plan | Breakfast | Lunch | Dinner | Motivational Quotes |
|---|---|---|---|---|
| Day-1 | Rolled Oats Cereal | One Pan Chicken | Butternut Squash and Apple Salad | It is never too late to make amends. |
| Day-2 | Rolled Oats Cereal | One Pan Chicken | Flavors Corn Soup | The net will appear if you leap. |
| Day-3 | Mocha Fruit Shake | Braised Celery Root | Mexican Skillet Meal | The key to change is to devote all of your energy to building the new rather than fighting the old. |
| Day-4 | Cranberry Hotcakes | Waldorf Salad with Yogurt | Mexican Skillet Meal | You get what you concentrate on, so concentrate on what you want. |
| Day-5 | Orange Mango Sunshine Smoothie | Chicken Pesto Baguette | Chicken Vegetable Stew | Yes, I believe I can. |
| Day-6 | Hummus and Date Bagel | Lean Beef Lettuce Wraps | Salmon Veggie Chowder | Don't give up until you're satisfied. |
| Day-7 | Protein Cereal | Lean Beef Lettuce Wraps | Zucchini Frittata | A small amount of progress each day adds up to big results. |

# Chapter 4
# Breakfast

## Vegetable Omelet

**Prep time: 5 minutes | Cook time: 5 minutes | Serves 2**

- 1/4 cup of onion; diced
- 1 tablespoon of olive oil
- 1/4 cup of green bell peppers; diced
- 2 ounces mushrooms; sliced
- 1/4 cup of zucchini; sliced
- 2 tablespoons of fat-free sour cream
- 1/2 cup of tomato; diced
- 2 ounces Swiss cheese; shredded
- 1 cup of egg substitute
- 2 tablespoons of water

1. In a large pan, heat the olive oil and cook the mushrooms, zucchini, green bell pepper, onion, and tomato until tender, finishing with the tomato.
2. Combine the sour cream egg substitute, and whisk until frothy. Place an omelet pan or skillet over medium-high heat and coat with the nonstick veggie spray.
3. Fill the pan with the egg mixture. As it cooks, lift the sides to enable the raw egg to flow below. Cover half of the eggs with cheese and sautéed veggies when almost set, then fold another half over. Cook the eggs until they are set.

**PER SERVING**

Calories: 263 kcal, Protein: 25 g, Carbohydrates: 8 g, Fat: 13 g, Cholesterol: 17 mg, Fiber: 2 g

## Breakfast Potatoes

**Prep time: 5 minutes | Cook time: 15 minutes | Serves 6**

- 1/4 cup of green bell peppers; chopped
- 1 cup of onion; chopped
- 4 potatoes
- 1/2 teaspoon of freshly ground black pepper
- 1 tablespoon of unsalted margarine

1. Potatoes are boiled or microwaved until nearly done. Drain them and, coarsely, chop them and combine them with onion & green bell pepper.
2. In a wide skillet, melt margarine. Toss in the potato mixture. Add a pinch of black pepper to the top. Fry till golden brown, flipping often.

**PER SERVING**

Calories: 201 kcal, Protein: 5 g, Carbohydrates: 42 g, Fat: 2 g, Cholesterol: 0 mg, Fiber: 5 g

## Couscous Cereal with Fruit

**Prep time: 5 minutes | Cook time: 5 minutes | Serves 2**

- 2 tablespoons of raisins
- 1/2 cup of couscous
- 3/4 cup of water
- 2 tablespoons of dried cranberries
- 1/2 teaspoon of cinnamon
- 1 tablespoon of honey

1. Bring a pot of water to a gentle boil. Stir in the couscous, then cover & remove from the heat.
2. Allow for a 5-minute rest period. Add the remaining ingredients.

**PER SERVING**

Calories: 250 kcal, Protein: 6 g, Carbohydrates: 57 g, Fat: 2 g, Cholesterol: 0 mg, Fiber: 3 g

## French Toast

**Prep time: 5 minutes | Cook time: 15 minutes | Serves 4**

- 3/4 cup of skim milk
- 1/2 cup of egg substitute
- 2 teaspoons of vanilla extract
- 8 slices of day-old, whole wheat bread
- 1/2 teaspoon of cinnamon

1. Whisk the egg substitute, vanilla, milk, and cinnamon in a large mixing bowl or dish. Dip both sides of the bread into the egg mixture.
2. Place a griddle or nonstick skillet over medium-high heat and coat with the nonstick vegetable oil spray.
3. Cook for at least 3 minutes on each side, or until both sides of bread are golden brown, on a pan or skillet.

**PER SERVING**

Calories: 185 kcal, Protein: 11 g, Carbohydrates: 27 g, Fat: 3 g, Cholesterol: 1 mg, Fiber: 2 g

## Pasta Frittata

**Prep time: 10 minutes | Cook time: 20 minutes |Serves 4**

- 1 cup of onion; chopped
- 2 tablespoons of olive oil
- 1 cup of red bell pepper; diced
- 2 cups of cooked pasta
- 1 cup of egg substitute
- 1/4 cup of grated Parmesan

1. Preheat a broiler-safe nonstick skillet with a 1 Q-inch (25-cm) diameter. When the pan is heated, add the oil, and cook the red bell pepper and onion, stirring regularly, for 2 to 3 minutes. Toss the pasta into the pan and toss thoroughly. F
2. latten the pasta onto the pan's bottom using a spatula when all the ingredients are fully mixed. Allow it to simmer for a few more minutes. Whisk the egg substitute and the grated Parmesan cheese in a separate bowl.
3. Pour the egg mixture over pasta, ensuring eggs are equally distributed. Lift the edges of the pasta gently to allow the egg to pour beneath and coat the pasta fully. Allow 6 to 9 minutes for the eggs to cook. Finish cooking by placing the pan on the hot broiler.

**PER SERVING**

Calories: 360 kcal, Protein: 18 g, Carbohydrates: 46 g, Fat: 12 g, Cholesterol: 6 mg, Fiber: 3 g

## Breakfast Quesadilla

**Prep time: 5 minutes | Cook time: 10 minutes |Serves 4**

- 1 cup of egg substitute
- 1/4 cup of salsa
- 1/4 cup of low-fat cheddar cheese; shredded
- 8 corn tortillas

1. Prepare the scrambled eggs, using egg replacer and when almost ready, mix in the salsa and cheese. Using a nonstick olive oil spray, lightly coat one side of the tortillas and arrange four of them oiled side down on a baking sheet.
2. Spread the egg mixture among the tortillas, smoothing it evenly. The remaining tortillas, oiled side up, go on top. Grill the quesadillas for 3 minutes on each side, or until golden brown. To serve, cut into quarters.

**PER SERVING**

Calories: 152 kcal, Protein: 12 g, Carbohydrates: 18 g, Fat: 4 g, Cholesterol: 2 mg, Fiber: 3 g

## Hummus and Date Bagel

**Prep time: 3 minutes | Cook time: 5 minutes |Serves 1**

- ¼ serving of Homemade Hummus/store-bought hummus
- 6 dates, pitted &halved
- 1 bagel
- Dash of salt & pepper to taste
- ¼ cup of diced tomatoes
- 1 tbsp. of chives
- A squeeze of lemon juice
- 1 handful sprouts

1. The bagel is split in half. In a toaster or under the broiler, toast the bagel. Each side is rubbed with hummus. Add the salt, dates, and pepper to taste.

**PER SERVING**

Calories: 410 kcal, Protein: 91 g, Carbohydrates: 59 g, Fat: 2 g, Cholesterol: 0 mg, Fiber: 9.7 g

## Curry Tofu Scramble

**Prep time: 5 minutes | Cook time: 5 minutes |Serves 3**

- 1 teaspoon of curry powder
- 1 teaspoon of olive oil
- 12oz. crumbled tofu
- ¼ cup of skim milk
- ¼ teaspoon of chili flakes

1. In a skillet, heat the olive oil. Toss in the tofu crumbles and chili flakes. Combine skim milk and curry powder in a mixing dish.
2. Stir thoroughly after pouring the liquid over crumbled tofu. On medium-high heat, scramble the tofu for 3 minutes.

**PER SERVING**

Calories: 102 kcal, Protein: 10 g, Carbohydrates: 3.3 g, Fat: 6.4 g, Cholesterol: 0 mg, Fiber: 3 g

## Breakfast Splits

**Prep time: 10 minutes | Cook time: 0 minutes |Serves 2**

- 2 tablespoons of low-fat yogurt
- 2 peeled bananas
- 4 tablespoons of granola
- 2 chopped strawberries
- ½ teaspoon of ground cinnamon

1. Combine yogurt, ground cinnamon, and strawberries in a mixing dish. Then cut the bananas lengthwise and fill them with the yogurt mass. Granola may be sprinkled on top of the fruits.

**PER SERVING**

Calories: 154 kcal, Protein: 6.8 g, Carbohydrates: 45.2 g, Fat: 8 g, Cholesterol: 1 mg, Fiber: 4 g

## Tomato Basil Bruschetta

**Prep time: 5 minutes | Cook time: 0 minutes |Serves 6**

- 2 tablespoons of chopped basil
- 1/2 whole-grain baguette, six 1/2-inch-thick diagonal slices
- 1 tablespoon of chopped parsley
- 3 diced tomatoes,
- 2 minced cloves garlic
- 1 teaspoon of olive oil
- 1/2 cup of diced fennel
- 1 teaspoon of black pepper
- 2 teaspoons of balsamic vinegar

1. Preheat the oven to 400 degrees Fahrenheit. Baguette pieces should be gently toasted. Combine all the remaining ingredients in a large mixing bowl.
2. Distribute the mixture equally over the toasted bread. Serve right away.

**PER SERVING**

Calories: 142 kcal, Protein: 5 g, Carbohydrates: 26 g, Fat: 2 g, Cholesterol: 0 mg, Fiber: 2 g

## Creamed Rice

**Prep time: 5 minutes | Cook time: 20 minutes | Serves 2**

- ½ cup brown basmati rice
- 2 cups water
- 1 cup unsweetened almond milk, plus extra for serving
- 1 tsp vanilla extract
- ⅛ tsp ground cinnamon
- Pinch fine sea salt
- ¼ cup dried raisins
- ¼ cup unsalted mixed nuts, chopped
- 2 tbsp. organic honey

1. Place the basmati rice in a large-sized mixing bowl and add the water. Soak overnight in the refrigerator, then drain.
2. Add the soaked rice, water, almond milk, vanilla extract, cinnamon, and fine sea salt in a medium-sized stockpot and place over medium heat.
3. Bring the rice mixture to a boil and then reduce the heat to low. Simmer for 20 minutes, until the rice is tender and most of the liquid has been absorbed, stirring frequently.
4. Remove the stockpot from the heat and mix in the raisins, nuts, and honey. Add extra almond milk if you prefer a thinner pudding.
5. Serve.

**PER SERVING**

Calories: 341; Total Fat: 8g; Saturated Fat: 0g; Cholesterol: 0mg; Sodium: 213mg; Total Carbs: 64g; Net Carbs: 24g; Protein: 6g

## Egg Foo Young

**Prep time: 5 minutes | Cook time: 10 minutes | Serves 3**

- Cooking spray
- ½ medium red bell pepper, chopped
- ½ medium green bell pepper, chopped
- ¼ cup red onion, finely chopped
- ¼ cup Roma tomatoes, chopped
- ¼ cup lean ham, chopped
- 2½ cups large egg whites
- ½ tsp basil, chopped
- Fine sea salt
- Ground black pepper

1. Spray a medium nonstick frying pan with cooking spray and place it over medium heat.
2. Add the red and green bell peppers, onion, tomato, and ham to the pan and fry for 4 minutes until tender.
3. Add the egg whites into the pan, over the ham mixture, and cook for 1 minute, until just beginning to set. Use a rubber spatula or turner and gently lift the edges of the setting egg whites, while tilting the pan to allow any uncooked egg to run beneath. Continue this process for 3 minutes until all the egg whites are set.
4. Remove the pan from the heat and fold one side of the egg white omelet over the other.
5. Cut the omelet in half and sprinkled with chopped basil and seasoned with fine sea salt and ground black pepper. Serve warm.

**PER SERVING**

Calories: 215; Total Fat: 2g; Saturated Fat: 0g; Cholesterol: 15mg; Sodium: 469mg; Total Carbs: 8g; Net Carbs: 1g; Protein: 40g

## Cranberry Hotcakes

**Prep time:** 5 minutes | **Cook time:** 9 minutes | **Serves 2**

- 1 cup rolled oats
- 1 cup cranberries
- 3 tbsp. fat-free plain yoghurt
- ¼ cup unsweetened almond milk
- 1 tbsp. ground flaxseed
- 1 large egg
- ½ tsp ground cinnamon
- 2 tsp avocado oil

1. In a medium-sized mixing bowl, mix the oats, cranberries, yoghurt, almond milk, flax seeds, egg, and cinnamon together, until it becomes a thick batter.
2. In a large nonstick frying pan, heat the avocado oil over medium-low heat. Pour ¼ cup of the batter into the pan and fry for 2 to 3 minutes, or until bubbles start to form on top, flip, and fry for 2 minutes, or until lightly browned and fully cooked. Continue with the remaining batter.
3. Serve with your favorite toppings.

**PER SERVING**

Calories: 328; Total Fat: 12g; Saturated Fat: 2g; Cholesterol: 83mg; Sodium: 54mg; Total Carbs: 43g; Net Carbs: 10g; Protein: 13g

## Avo Bruschetta

**Prep time:** 5 minutes | **Cook time:** 5 minutes | **Serves 2**

- 1 tbsp. olive oil
- 2 large free-range eggs
- 1 ripe avocado, pitted, peeled, and mashed
- 2 whole-wheat bread small slices, toasted
- Fine sea salt
- Ground black pepper
- Pinch red pepper flakes, (optional)
- 1 large Roma tomato, thinly sliced

1. Heat the olive oil in a medium-sized nonstick frying pan over medium heat.
2. Gently crack the eggs into the pan and fry for 3 to 4 minutes, flip, and cook for an extra 30 seconds, or until it has reached your desired doneness. Remove from the heat.
3. Portion the avocado evenly between the toasted slices, season with salt, pepper, and a pinch of red pepper flakes (if using).
4. Place the sliced tomatoes over the avocado, top with the fried egg, and enjoy.

**PER SERVING**

Calories: 411; Total Fat: 28g; Saturated Fat: 6g; Sodium: 302mg; Total Carbs: 29g; Protein: 14g

## Vegetarian Scramble

**Prep time:** 5 minutes | **Cook time:** 15 minutes | **Serves 1**

- 2 tsp olive oil
- ¼ cup red onion, chopped
- 1 cup cherry tomatoes, halved
- 1 cup baby spinach
- 10 oz firm tofu, crumbled
- ¼ cup low-fat cottage cheese
- 1 tsp oregano, chopped
- Himalayan pink salt
- Ground black pepper

1. Heat the olive oil in a medium nonstick frypan over medium heat.
2. Add the chopped onion to the pan and fry for 3 minutes until translucent.
3. Add the tomato halves and baby spinach, fry for 3 minutes until the spinach is wilted.
4. Add the tofu to the pan and gently mix using a rubber spatula for 7 minutes until warmed through.
5. Gently mix in the cottage cheese and oregano.
6. Season with salt and pepper, serve warm.

**PER SERVING**

Calories: 201; Total Fat: 5g; Saturated Fat: 1g; Cholesterol: 2mg; Sodium: 97mg; Total Carbs: 9g; Net Carbs: 4g; Protein: 20g

## Rolled Oats Cereal

**Prep time:** 5 minutes | **Cook time:** 5 minutes | **Serves 4**

- 2 tbsp. plant-based butter, plus 1 tablespoon unsalted butter
- 1 tbsp. organic honey
- ¾ cup rolled oats
- ⅓ cup walnuts, roughly chopped
- 1 tbsp. chia seeds
- 1 tbsp. hemp seeds
- 1 tbsp. ground flaxseed
- ½ tsp ground cinnamon
- Pinch fine sea salt
- 2 tbsp. dried cranberries
- 2 tbsp. raisins

1. In a large heavy bottom pan, melt the butter and honey over medium heat, cook until bubbly.
2. Mix in the oats, walnuts, chia seeds, hemp seeds, flaxseed, cinnamon, and salt. Cook for 3 to 4 minutes, stirring until the oats and nuts start to brown. If the mixture is browning too fast, turn the heat down to low. Remove from the heat and add the cranberries and raisins, mix to combine.
3. Eat the oat cereal right away or cool it completely, then store it in an airtight container.

**PER SERVING**

Calories: 230; Total Fat: 16g; Saturated Fat: 3g; Cholesterol: 8mg; Sodium: 64mg; Total Carbs: 18g; Protein: 5g

## Italian Baked Omelet
Prep time: 5 minutes | Cook time: 20 minutes | Serves 2

- Cooking spray
- 6 large free-range egg whites
- ¼ cup unsweetened soy milk
- ½ tsp basil, chopped
- Himalayan pink salt
- Ground black pepper
- ¼ cup green beans, chopped
- ¼ cup red bell pepper, chopped
- ½ spring onion, chopped
- 2 tbsp. fat-free cheddar cheese, shredded

1. Preheat the oven to 350°F gas mark 4. Grease 2 medium ramekins with cooking spray and set aside.
2. In a medium-sized mixing bowl, add the egg whites, soy milk, and basil, whisk until well blended. Season with salt and pepper, set aside.
3. Divide the green beans, red bell pepper, and spring onion between the 2 ramekins and pour in the egg white mixture. Top each ramekin with 1 tbsp. of cheddar cheese.
4. Bake for 15 to 20 minutes, until the baked omelet has puffed up and lightly browned. Serve hot.

**PER SERVING**

Calories: 126; Total Fat: 4g; Saturated Fat: 2g; Cholesterol: 10mg; Sodium: 164mg; Total Carbs: 5g; Net Carbs: 2g; Protein: 16g

## Nutty Oat Cereal
Prep time: 5 minutes | Cook time: 30 minutes | Serves 4

- Parchment paper
- 1 cup rolled oats
- 1 cup dried pumpkin seeds
- ½ cup unsalted mixed nuts, roughly chopped
- Pinch fine sea salt
- 1 tbsp. olive oil
- 2 cups unsweetened cashew milk
- 1 cup strawberries, chopped
- 1 cup blueberries

1. Heat the oven to 300°F gas mark 2. Line a baking sheet with parchment paper.
2. In a medium-sized mixing bowl, add the oats, pumpkin seeds, mixed nuts, salt, and olive oil, mix to combine.
3. Transfer the oat mixture onto the prepared baking sheet in a thin layer.
4. Bake for 30 minutes, mixing the oats halfway through cooking, until lightly browned. Remove and set aside to cool.
5. Serve with cashew milk, chopped strawberries, and blueberries.

**PER SERVING**

Calories: 460; Total Fat: 32g; Saturated Fat: 3g; Sodium: 106mg; Total Carbs: 34g; Protein: 14g

## Protein Cereal
Prep time: 5 minutes | Cook time: 20 minutes | Serves 4

- 1¾ cups water
- 1 cup quinoa
- Pinch fine sea salt
- 1 cup raisins
- ½ cup almonds, roughly chopped
- 1 cup unsweetened almond milk
- 4 tsp organic honey

1. In a medium stockpot, add the water, quinoa, and salt, allow to boil.
2. Bring the heat down to low and simmer, covered, for 15 minutes, or until the water is absorbed. Remove from the heat and let it rest for 5 minutes.
3. Add the raisins and almonds, mix to combine.
4. Place a ¾ cup of the quinoa mixture into 4 bowls and pour a ¼ cup of almond milk in each bowl. Drizzle each bowl of quinoa with 1 tsp of organic honey.

**PER SERVING**

Calories: 313; Total Fat: 10g; Saturated Fat: 1g; Sodium: 33mg; Total Carbs: 48g; Protein: 10g

## Maghrebi Poached Eggs
Prep time: 5 minutes | Cook time: 25 minutes | Serves 4

- 1 tbsp. avocado oil
- 1 medium red bell pepper, chopped
- 1 (28 oz) can low-sodium diced tomatoes
- 1 tsp ground cumin
- Fine sea salt
- Ground black pepper
- 4 large free-range eggs
- ¼ cup cilantro, chopped

1. Heat the avocado oil in a large heavy-bottom pan over medium-high heat.
2. Add the red bell pepper and cook for 4 to 6 minutes, until softened.
3. Add the tomatoes with the juice and cumin. Cook for 10 minutes, or until the flavor comes together and the sauce has thickened. Season with salt and pepper to taste.
4. Use a large spoon to make 4 depressions in the tomato mixture. Carefully crack an egg into each depression. Cover the pan and cook for 5 to 7 minutes, or until the eggs are cooked to your liking. Remove from the heat.
5. Divide into 4 bowls and garnish with chopped cilantro. Serve while hot.

**PER SERVING**

Calories: 146; Total Fat: 9g; Saturated Fat: 2g; Sodium: 102mg; Total Carbs: 10g; Protein: 8g

# Chapter 5
# Smoothies and Drinks

## Mango Oat Smoothie

**Prep time:5 minutes| Cook time:0 minutes| Serves 3**

- 1/4 cup of old-fashioned oats
- 2 cups of frozen mango
- 1 banana: (frozen is better)
- 2 cups of oat milk /other plant-based milk /skim milk
- 1/4 lemon/orange (juiced)
- 1 tablespoon of ground flaxseed

1. In a blender, combine all of the ingredients. Blend until completely smooth. Pour into three glasses and enjoy!

**PER SERVING**

Calories: 201 kcal, Protein: 8 g, Carbohydrates: 39 g, Fat: 3 g, Cholesterol: 3 mg, Fiber: 4 g

## Avocado Island Green Smoothie

**Prep time:5 minutes| Cook time:0 minutes| Serves 1**

- ¼ medium avocado
- ½ cup of coconut milk
- 5.3-ounce coconut yogurt
- ½ cup of frozen pineapple
- 1 cup of power greens (any leafy greens)
- 1 tbsp. of ground flaxseed

**GARNISHES**

- Optional: 1 wedge of fresh pineapple
- ½ tbsp. of shredded coconut optional

1. Simply combine the ingredients in a blender and mix until smooth.

**PER SERVING**

Calories: 339 kcal, Protein: 19 g, Carbohydrates: 34 g, Fat: 16 g, Cholesterol: 10 mg, Fiber: 8 g

## Pumpkin Pie Smoothie

**Prep time:5 minutes| Cook time:0 minutes| Serves 1**

1 medium frozen banana
1 cup of light vanilla almond milk or milk of choice
1/4 cup of ice
1/2 tsp of pumpkin pie spice
1 scoop of vanilla protein powder
1/8 tsp of cinnamon
1 tbsp. of almond butter
1/4 cup of canned pumpkin puree

1. Simply combine the ingredients in a blender and mix until smooth.

**PER SERVING**

Calories: 393 kcal, Protein: 30 g, Carbohydrates: 49 g, Fat: 12 g, Cholesterol: 40 mg, Fiber: 6 g

## Cashew & Berry Shake

**Prep time: 5 minutes | Serves 2**

- 2 cups fresh or frozen berries (your choice)
- 1¾ cups unsweetened cashew milk
- 1 cup fresh or frozen spinach, roughly chopped
- ¼ cup cashew butter
- ½ cup ice cubes

1. In a blender, add the berries of choice, cashew milk, spinach, and cashew butter. Blend until lump-free and smooth.
2. Add the ice cubes and blend until smooth.

**PER SERVING**

Calories: 324; Total Fat: 22g; Saturated Fat: 1g; Sodium: 186mg; Total Carbs: 29g; Protein: 11g

## Vegan Tropical Smoothie

**Prep time:5 minutes| Cook time:0 minutes | Serves 2**

- 1 large frozen banana
- ¼ cup of Silken tofu
- 1 cup of almond milk
- 1 ½ cup of frozen strawberries
- 1½ cup of frozen mango¼ cup of water (more or less may require depending on preference)
- 2 Tbsp. of hemp seeds

1. Toss all ingredients into a blender, except the water, and mix until desired consistency is reached.

**PER SERVING**

Calories: 279 kcal, Protein: 3 g, Carbohydrates: 39 g, Fat: 15 g, Cholesterol: 9 mg, Fiber: 5 g

## Strawberry Rhubarb Pie Smoothie

**Prep time:5 minutes| Cook time:0 minutes| Serves 1**

- 1/2 cup of chopped rhubarb
- 1 cup of frozen sliced strawberries
- 1 small or 1/2 medium banana; (1/2 cup of sliced), ideally frozen
- 3 tablespoons of rolled oats
- 1 tablespoon of slivered almonds
- 1 tablespoon of maple syrup
- Optional: nutty granola; for topping
- 1 cup of unsweetened coconut milk beverage
- Ice, as needed
- 1 teaspoon of vanilla

1. Combine all ingredients in a blender and blend until smooth. As required, add ice to the mix. Top with your favorite nutty granola, if desired.

**PER SERVING**

Calories: 372 kcal, Protein: 8 g, Carbohydrates: 31 g, Fat: 27 g, Cholesterol: 10 mg, Fiber: 4 g

## Mocha Fruit Shake

**Prep time: 10 minutes | Serves 2**

- 1 medium frozen banana
- 1 cup baby spinach
- 1 cup frozen strawberries
- 2 tbsp. unsweetened cocoa powder
- 1 cup brewed coffee, chilled
- 1½ cups vanilla almond milk
- 1 tbsp. flaxseed
- ¼ to ½ cup water (optional)

1. Place the banana in a blender and blend it into smaller pieces.
2. In the blender, add the baby spinach, strawberries, cocoa powder, coffee, almond milk, and flax seeds, blend until smooth. Add the water a few tbsp. at a time, if you prefer a thinner shake.

**PER SERVING**

Calories: 285; Total Fat: 13g; Saturated Fat: 2g; Cholesterol: 0mg; Sodium: 180mg; Total Carbs: 37g; Net Carbs: 5g; Protein: 12g

## Berry Coconut Water Smoothie

**Prep time:5 minutes| Cook time:0 minutes| Serves 2**

- 2 tablespoons of warm water
- ¼ cup of goji berries
- 3 cups of frozen berries
- 1 teaspoon of ground cinnamon
- 1 cup of unsweetened coconut milk/ yogurt alternative
- 1 banana
- 1 cup of coconut water

**OPTIONAL FOR SERVING:**
- Fresh berries
- Granola; (homemade/store-bought)

1. In a blender container, combine the goji berries and water and mix for 30 seconds, or until smooth. If necessary, scrape down the sides of the blender with a spatula.
2. Blend on high for 2 minutes, or until smooth and creamy, adding coconut milk/yogurt alternatives, coconut water, banana, frozen berries, and cinnamon to the blender container. Transfer to glasses and, if preferred, top with granola and fresh berries.

**PER SERVING**

Calories: 390 kcal, Protein: 5.3 g, Carbohydrates: 59.6 g, Fat: 5.3 g, Cholesterol: 10 mg, Fiber: 14.2 g

## Orange Mango Sunshine Smoothie

**Prep time:5 minutes| Cook time:5 minutes| Serves 2**

- 1 mango (2 cups; cubes)
- 2 oranges; segments only
- 1 medium carrot
- 1/2-1 tsp of minced, fresh ginger
- 1 cup of unsweetened soy milk/milk of choice
- 1 cup of ice
- 1/4 tsp of turmeric

1. Blend all the ingredients in a high-powered blender until smooth. If preferred, top with a sprinkling of cinnamon.

**PER SERVING**

Calories: 248 kcal, Protein: 6.7 g, Carbohydrates: 54.4 g, Fat: 2.9 g, Cholesterol: 0 mg, Fiber: 7.8 g

## Banana Nut Smoothie

**Prep time:5 minutes| Cook time: | Serves 1**

- 2 tbsp. of almond butter
- 1 banana
- 1/2 tsp of cinnamon
- 1 cup of almond milk
- 1 tsp of maple syrup
- 1 tbsp. of flaxseed; (optional)

1. Combine all ingredients in a blender and blend until smooth. If desired, sprinkle with cinnamon. Serve right away.

**PER SERVING**

Calories: 412 kcal, Protein: 11 g, Carbohydrates: 43 g, Fat: 25 g, Cholesterol: 2.5 mg, Fiber: 11 g

## Carrot Banana Smoothie

**Prep time:5 minutes| Cook time:0 minutes| Serves 1**

- ¼ cup of oats
- 1 cup of dairy-free milk: protein added milk /soy milk
- ⅓ cup of shredded carrots
- 1 tablespoon of walnuts
- 1 tablespoon of raisins
- ½ frozen banana; about ½ cup of frozen slices
- 1 tablespoon of ground flaxseed
- 1 scoop of vanilla protein powder
- 1 teaspoon of ground cinnamon

1. Combine all ingredients except the protein powder and frozen bananas in a blender. Stir or shake the mixture and set aside for 10 minutes.
2. Combine the protein powder with the frozen bananas. Blend until the mixture is smooth and creamy.

**PER SERVING**

Calories: 379 kcal, Protein: 25 g, Carbohydrates: 40 g, Fat: 16 g, Cholesterol: 0 mg, Fiber: 11 g

## Healthy Blueberry Smoothie with Almond Butter

**Prep time:3 minutes| Cook time:0 minutes| Serves 1**

- 1/2 banana
- 1/2 cup of blueberries
- 1 tbsp. of almond butter
- 6 oz. vanilla soy milk
- 1 tbsp. of cocoa powder
- ¼ teaspoon of cinnamon
- ½ cup of ice chips
- 1 tbsp. of flaxseed

1. In a blender cup, combine all of the ingredients. Blend for 10 seconds or until the mixture is completely smooth.

### PER SERVING

Calories: 338 kcal, Protein: 11.7 g, Carbohydrates: 42.9 g, Fat: 16.7 g, Cholesterol: 0 mg, Fiber: 10.8 g

## Morning Glory Smoothie

**Prep time:5 minutes|Cook time:0 minutes | Serves 2**

- 1 cup of milk
- ½ cup of apple juice
- 2 tablespoons of walnuts
- 2 tablespoons of unsweetened coconut flakes
- 2 frozen bananas
- 1 small carrot
- ½ teaspoon ground cinnamon
- ½ teaspoon of pure vanilla extract
- ½ teaspoon of stevia
- 1-2 cups of ice cubes

1. Combine the milk, walnuts, apple juice, and coconut flakes in a blender mixer. Allow for 5 minutes of resting time.
2. Add the frozen bananas, cinnamon, carrots, stevia, vanilla essence, and ice cubes in a pitcher. Puree until completely smooth. Serve right away.

### PER SERVING

Calories: 276 kcal, Protein: 6 g, Carbohydrates: 46 g, Fat: 8 g, Cholesterol: 2 mg, Fiber: 6 g

## Celery Smoothie with Apple and Banana

**Prep time:5 minutes| Cook time:0 minutes | Serves 2**

- 1 cup of baby spinach
- 1 cup of chopped celery: preferably frozen
- 1 green apple: cored & cut into chunks
- 1 frozen banana
- ½ avocado
- 1 tablespoon lemon juice
- Dash of vanilla extract
- 1 teaspoon of freshly grated ginger

1. Combine all ingredients in a blender. Add about ¾ to 1 cup water. Blend until smooth, and enjoy!

### PER SERVING

Calories: 194 kcal, Protein: 3 g, Carbohydrates: 33 g, Fat: 8 g, Cholesterol: 1 mg, Fiber: 8 g

## Green Smoothie with Chia and Peach

**Prep time:5 minutes| Cook time:0 minutes | Serves 2**

- 1 tbsp. of chia seeds
- 1 banana, ideally frozen
- 1 peach chopped, ripe
- 1 cup of cold unsweetened almond milk
- 1 cup of fresh, washed spinach

1. In a blender, combine the ingredients in the order stated (you want your greens on the bottom by the blade, so they blend better and have the chia on the bottom to absorb some liquid before you blend).
2. Allow for a few minutes for the chia seeds to absorb the almond milk. Combine all ingredients in a blender and serve with your preferred toppings. Enjoy!

### PER SERVING

Calories: 241 kcal, Protein: 6 g, Carbohydrates: 43 g, Fat: 7 g, Cholesterol: 1 mg, Fiber: 10 g.

# Chapter 6
# Poultry

## Chicken, Mushroom, and Bell Pepper Skewers

**Prep time: 10 minutes | Cook time: 17 minutes | Serves 4**

- 1 pound skinless, boneless chicken breast, cut into 1-inch cubes
- ⅓ cup Oregano-Thyme Sauce
- 2 bell peppers, cut into 1-inch chunks
- 24 whole white mushrooms
- 1 tablespoon minced garlic
- 1½ tablespoons olive oil
- Sea salt

1. Preheat the oven to 450°F. Line a baking sheet with parchment paper.
2. In a medium bowl, toss the chicken breast with the Oregano-Thyme Sauce.
3. Thread the chicken, peppers, and mushrooms onto 8 wooden or metal skewers. (If using wooden skewers, be sure to soak them for 30 minutes beforehand.)
4. Place the skewers on the prepared baking sheet and bake for about 17 minutes, until the chicken edges are slightly brown and it is cooked to an internal temperature of 165°F. Serve immediately.

**PER SERVING (2 SKEWERS)**

Calories: 191; Total fat: 7g; Saturated fat: 1g; Trans fat: 0g; Protein: 24g; Total carbohydrate: 8g; Fiber: 2g; Sodium: 313mg; Potassium: 685mg

## Lemon Chicken and Asparagus

**Prep time: 10 minutes, plus 30 minutes to marinate | Cook time: 20 minutes | Serves 4**

- 1 pound boneless, skinless chicken thighs, cut into 1-inch pieces
- ½ cup Lemon-Garlic Sauce
- 2½ cups (about 1 pound) chopped asparagus
- 1 tablespoon minced garlic
- 1½ tablespoons olive oil
- Sea salt
- Freshly ground black pepper

1. Place the chicken and Lemon-Garlic Sauce in a resealable plastic bag and marinate in the refrigerator for 30 minutes or overnight.
2. In a medium bowl, toss the asparagus with the garlic and olive oil, and season with salt and pepper.
3. In a large skillet over high heat, sauté the chicken until cooked through and browned, about 15 minutes. Transfer the chicken with a slotted spoon to a plate and set aside.
4. Add the asparagus to the skillet and sauté until tender-crisp, about 5 minutes. Enjoy immediately.

**PER SERVING (3 OUNCES OF CHICKEN AND ½ CUP ASPARAGUS)**

Calories: 221; Total fat: 13g; Saturated fat: 3g; Trans fat: 0g; Protein: 20g; Total carbohydrate: 6g; Fiber: 2g; Sodium: 352mg; Potassium: 437mg

## Spicy Honey Chicken and Eggplant

**Prep time: 10 minutes, plus 30 minutes to marinate | Cook time: 30 minutes | Serves 4**

- 1 pound boneless, skinless chicken thighs
- ⅓ cup Spicy Honey Sauce
- 2 eggplants, cut into ¼-inch-thick slices
- 2 tablespoons minced garlic
- Sea salt
- Freshly ground black pepper

1. Place the chicken and the Spicy Honey Sauce in a resealable plastic bag, and marinate in the refrigerator for 30 minutes or overnight.
2. Preheat the oven to 400°F. Line a baking sheet with parchment paper.
3. Place the eggplant slices on half of the prepared baking sheet, sprinkle them with the garlic, and season them with salt and pepper.
4. Cook until the eggplant is caramelized and the chicken reaches an internal temperature of 165°F, about 25 to 30 minutes. Serve immediately.

**PER SERVING (3 OUNCES OF CHICKEN AND ½ CUP EGGPLANT)**

Calories: 248; Total fat: 10g; Saturated fat: 1g; Trans fat: 0g; Protein: 20g; Total carbohydrate: 21g; Fiber: 8g; Sodium: 370mg; Potassium: 741mg

## Sweet Salad Dressing Chicken and Carrot Sheet Pan Dinner

**Prep time: 5 minutes, plus 30 minutes to marinate | Cook time: 25 minutes | Serves 4**

- 1 pound boneless, skinless chicken thighs
- ½ cup Sweet Salad Dressing
- 2½ cups carrots cut into thin matchsticks
- 1½ tablespoons olive oil
- 1 tablespoon minced garlic
- Sea salt
- Freshly ground black pepper

1. Place the chicken and Sweet Salad Dressing in a resealable plastic bag and marinate for 30 minutes or overnight in the refrigerator.
2. Preheat the oven to 425°F. Line a baking sheet with parchment.
3. In a medium bowl, toss the carrots with the olive oil and garlic, season with salt and pepper, and set aside.
4. After 5 minutes, add the carrots to the other side of the baking sheet and bake them with the chicken for the remaining 20 minutes, flipping the carrots halfway through. Enjoy immediately.

**PER SERVING (3 OUNCES OF CHICKEN AND ½ CUP CARROTS)**

Calories: 213; Total fat: 8g; Saturated fat: 2g; Trans fat: 0g; Protein: 19g; Total carbohydrate: 17g; Fiber: 2g; Sodium: 298mg; Potassium: 553mg

## Chicken Curry

**Prep time: 5 minutes | Cook time: 15 minutes | Serves 4**

- 1 tablespoon olive oil
- 1 pound boneless, skinless chicken thighs, thinly sliced
- 1 tablespoon minced garlic
- 1 white onion, diced
- 2 tablespoons curry powder
- ½ cup fat-free plain Greek yogurt
- Pinch sea salt

1. In a large skillet over medium heat, heat the olive oil and cook the chicken and garlic until the chicken is cooked through, about 10 minutes.
2. Add the onion and cook until it is translucent, about 5 minutes.
3. Add the curry powder and stir for 1 to 2 minutes until it is fragrant.
4. Remove the skillet from the heat, stir in the yogurt, and season with a pinch of salt. Serve immediately.

### PER SERVING (3 OUNCES)

Calories: 160; Total fat: 7g; Saturated fat: 1g; Trans fat: 0g; Protein: 20g; Total carbohydrate: 4g; Fiber: 2g; Sodium: 124mg; Potassium: 304mg

## Chicken Rice

**Prep time: 15 minutes | Cook time: 15 minutes| Serves 3**

- 1 cup brown basmati rice, cooked
- 1 cup chicken breast, cooked and chopped
- 1 cup spinach, cooked and shredded
- ½ cup low-sodium canned garbanzo beans, drained and rinsed
- 4 tbsp. lemon and herb vinaigrette, divided
- 1 large carrot, peeled and grated
- 1 large red bell pepper, diced
- 1 large green bell pepper, diced
- 1 cup frozen peas, cooked
- ½ cup frozen corn, cooked
- ¼ cup pine nuts, toasted for garnish

1. In a medium-sized mixing bowl, add the basmati rice, chicken breasts, spinach, garbanzo beans and 2 tbsp. of the lemon and herb vinaigrette, mix to combine.
2. Divide the rice mixture between two large bowls and arrange the carrot, red bell pepper, green bell pepper, peas, and corn in the bowls and drizzle with the remaining lemon and herb vinaigrette.
3. Top with pine nuts and serve.

### PER SERVING

Calories: 503; Total Fat: 21g; Saturated Fat: 3g; Cholesterol: 54mg; Sodium: 187mg; Total Carbs: 53g; Net Carbs: 13g; Protein: 32g

## Piña Colada Chicken

**Prep time: 5 minutes | Cook time: 20 minutes | Serves 2**

- Aluminum foil
- 2 (4 oz) chicken breasts, pounded flat
- 2 tsp unsweetened coconut flakes
- 1 (20 oz) can crushed pineapple, drained
- 1 cup green bell peppers, diced
- ¼ cup soy sauce

1. Heat the oven to 400°F gas mark 6. Line a baking sheet with aluminum foil.
2. Place the chicken breasts on the baking sheet and top with coconut flakes.
3. Place the pineapple and green bell peppers around the chicken breasts.
4. Drizzle the chicken breasts with soy sauce and cook for 10 to 15 minutes, until the pineapple is caramelised, and the chicken is cooked through. Serve warm.

### PER SERVING

Calories: 327, Total Fat: 6g, Saturated Fat: 1g, Cholesterol: 80mg, Sodium: 206mg, Total Carbs: 23g, Net Carbs: 24g, Protein: 31g

## Iron Packed Turkey

**Prep time: 5 minutes | Cook time: 30 minutes | Serves 2**

- 2 (3 oz) turkey breasts, boneless and skinless
- Himalayan pink salt
- Ground black pepper
- 3 tsp avocado oil, divided
- 1½ cups spinach, roughly chopped
- 1½ cups kale, roughly chopped
- 1½ cups Swiss chard, roughly chopped
- 1½ cups collard greens, roughly chopped
- 1 tsp garlic crushed

1. Preheat the oven to 400°F gas mark 6.
2. Season the turkey breasts with salt and pepper to taste.
3. Heat 1 tsp of avocado oil in a large cast-iron frying pan over medium-high heat.
4. Add the turkey breasts and cook for 5 minutes on each side until browned. Remove the turkey breasts and set them aside.
5. Add the remaining 2 tsp of avocado oil to the pan and fry the spinach, kale, Swiss chard, collard greens and garlic for 3 minutes until they are slightly wilted.
6. Season the mixed greens with salt and pepper to taste, place the turkey breasts on the greens.
7. Place the cast iron frying pan in the oven and bake for 15 minutes until the turkey breasts are cooked through.
8. Serve warm.

### PER SERVING

Calories: 113; Total Fat: 2g; Saturated Fat: 0g; Cholesterol: 49mg; Sodium: 128mg; Total Carbs: 4g; Net Carbs: 0g; Protein: 22g

## Lime Chicken Wraps

**Prep time: 5 minutes | Serves 2**

- 1 cup chicken breasts, cooked and chopped
- 1 cup low-sodium canned kidney beans, rinsed and drained
- ½ ripe avocado, diced
- 1 spring onion, finely chopped
- ½ lime, juiced and zested
- 1 tsp parsley, finely chopped
- ¼ tsp ground cumin
- 4 large iceberg lettuce leaves

1. In a medium-sized mixing bowl, add the chicken breasts, kidney beans, avocado, spring onion, lime juice and zest, parsley, and d cumin, mix until well combined.
2. Divide the chicken filling evenly between the lettuce leaves and roll closed.
3. Serve cold.

**PER SERVING**

Calories: 368; Total Fat: 11g; Saturated Fat: 2g; Cholesterol: 53mg; Sodium: 58mg; Total Carbs: 40g; Net Carbs: 13g; Protein: 30g

## Mediterranean Patties

**Prep time: 15 minutes | Cook time: 15 minutes | Serves 4**

- Aluminium foil
- 1 cup broccoli florets
- 1 small red onion, quartered
- ¼ cup black olives, pitted
- 8 oz baby spinach, roughly chopped
- 1 lb. ground chicken
- 1½ tsp mediterranean seasoning rub blend
- 4 whole wheat buns
- lettuce
- tomato

1. Preheat the oven to broil. Line a baking sheet with aluminum foil.
2. In a food processor, pulse the broccoli, onion, and olives for 1 to 2 minutes, until minced.
3. In a large-sized mixing bowl, add the baby spinach, broccoli mixture, chicken, and the Mediterranean spice blend, mix to combine. Form into 8 medium-sized patties and place them on the baking sheet.
4. Broil for 10 minutes on one side, flip, then broil for 3 minutes on the other side until golden brown.
5. Serve on wholewheat buns with lettuce and tomato, or with a garden salad.

**PER SERVING (2 BURGERS):**

Calories: 206, Total Fat: 10g, Saturated Fat: 3g, Cholesterol: 84mg, Sodium: 134mg, Total Carbs: 7g, Net Carbs: 2g, Protein: 25g

## Lime Turkey Skewers

**Prep time: 5 minutes | Cook time: 15 minutes | Serves 4**

- 1 lb. boneless, skinless turkey breasts, cut into chunks
- 1 lime, juiced
- 2 tbsp. avocado oil, plus 1 tbsp.
- 2 tbsp. garlic, minced
- 1 tsp dried thyme
- 1 tsp dried dill
- ½ tsp fine sea salt
- ¼ tsp ground black pepper

1. In a medium-sized mixing bowl, add the turkey breasts, lime juice, avocado oil, garlic, thyme, dill, salt and pepper, mix to combine. Rest for 30 minutes in the fridge.
2. Thread the marinated turkey chunks onto 8 skewers.
3. Heat 1 tbsp. of avocado oil in a heavy-bottom pan over medium-high heat.
4. Place the skewers gently in the pan and fry for 5 to 7 minutes, flip, and cook for 5 to 8 minutes, or until the turkey is cooked through and no longer pink inside. Remove from the heat and serve.

**PER SERVING**

Calories: 205; Total Fat: 10g; Saturated Fat: 2g; Sodium: 343mg; Total Carbs: 2g; Protein: 26g

## Italian Chicken Bake

**Prep time: 5 minutes | Cook time: 25 minutes | Serves 4**

- 1 lb. chicken breasts, halved lengthwise into 4 pieces
- ½ tsp garlic powder
- ½ tsp fine sea salt
- ¼ tsp ground black pepper
- ¼ tsp Italian seasoning
- ½ cup basil, finely chopped
- 4 part-skim mozzarella cheese slices
- 2 large Roma tomatoes, finely chopped

1. Heat the oven to 400°F gas mark 6.
2. Season the cut chicken breasts with garlic powder, salt, pepper and Italian seasoning.
3. Place the seasoned chicken breasts on a baking sheet. Bake for 18 to 22 minutes, or until the chicken breasts are cooked through. Remove from the oven and set it to broil on high.
4. Evenly place the basil, 1 mozzarella slice and tomatoes on each chicken breast.
5. Return the baking sheet to the oven and broil for 2 to 3 minutes, until the cheese has melted and browned.
6. Remove from the oven and serve hot.

**PER SERVING**

Calories: 239; Total Fat: 9g; Saturated Fat: 4g; Sodium: 524mg; Total Carbs: 4g; Protein: 33g

## One Pan Chicken

**Prep time: 5 minutes | Cook time: 30 minutes | Serves 4**

- 2 tbsp. olive oil
- 4 bone-in chicken thighs, skin removed
- ¾ tsp Himalayan pink salt, divided
- ½ tsp ground black pepper, divided
- 1 (15 oz) can petite diced tomatoes, drained
- ¼ cup water
- 1 (14 oz) can asparagus cut spears, drained
- ¼ cup black olives, pitted
- ¼ cup cilantro, chopped

1. Heat the oven to 350°F gas mark 4.
2. Heat the olive oil in a large oven-proof frying pan over a medium-high heat.
3. Season the chicken thighs with ¼ tsp of salt and ¼ tsp of pepper. Place the thighs in the frying pan and cook for 2 to 3 minutes per side, or until lightly browned, transfer to a plate.
4. In the same pan add the drained tomatoes and water and deglaze by scraping the bottom bits from the pan.
5. Add the asparagus, black olives, ½ tsp salt and ¼ tsp pepper, mix to combine.
6. Place the chicken thighs back into the pan and push them down into the tomato mixture.
7. Place the ovenproof pan in the oven and bake for 20 minutes, or until the chicken is fully cooked.
8. Remove from the oven and sprinkle with cilantro, serve warm.

**PER SERVING**

Calories: 270; Total Fat: 13g; Saturated Fat: 2g; Sodium: 514mg; Total Carbs: 15g; Protein: 26g

## Cashew Chicken

**Prep time: 5 minutes | Cook time: 5 minutes | Serves 2**

- 2 tsp olive oil
- 2 tsp garlic, minced, divided
- ½ cup red onion, chopped
- 8 oz ground chicken
- 1 tsp ginger, grated
- 3 tbsp. unsalted cashew butter
- 4 tbsp. water
- 6 large green leaf lettuce leaves
- ½ cup unsalted cashew nuts, roughly chopped

1. Heat the olive oil in a medium-sized frying pan over medium heat. Add the 1 tsp garlic and onion, cook for 1 to 2 minutes, until translucent.
2. Add the chicken and separate using a fork. Continue mixing for 5 minutes until lightly golden and cooked through.
3. In a small-sized mixing bowl, add the ginger, remaining 1 tsp garlic, cashew butter, and water, mix to combine.
4. Add the cashew mixture to the ground chicken. Cook for 1 minute until all flavors have combined.

5. Divide the cashew chicken mixture into the lettuce cups and serve topped with the cashew nuts.

**PER SERVING**

Calories: 414; Total Fat: 21g; Saturated Fat: 4g; Cholesterol: 90mg; Sodium: 211mg; Total Carbs: 17g; Net Carbs: 7g; Protein: 32g

## Balsamic Blueberry Chicken

**Prep time: 5 minutes | Cook time: 25 minutes | Serves 2**

- Aluminum foil
- ½ cup fresh blueberries
- 2 tbsp. pine nuts
- ¼ cup cilantro, chopped
- 2 tbsp. balsamic vinegar
- ¼ tsp ground black pepper
- 2 (4 oz) chicken breasts, butterflied

1. Heat the oven to 375°F gas mark 5. Line a baking sheet with aluminum foil.
2. In a medium-sized mixing bowl, add the blueberries, pine nuts, cilantro, balsamic vinegar, and pepper, mix until well combined.
3. Place the chicken breasts on the baking sheet and pour the blueberry mixture on top.
4. Bake for 20 to 25 minutes, until the juices are caramelized, and the inside of the chicken has cooked through. Serve warm.

**PER SERVING**

Calories: 212; Total Fat: 7g; Saturated Fat: 1g; Cholesterol: 80mg; Sodium: 58mg; Total Carbs: 11g; Net Carbs: 7g; Protein: 27g

## Red Wine Chicken

**Prep time: 5 minutes | Cook time: 30 minutes | Serves 4**

- 2 tbsp. plant-based butter, plus 1 tbsp. olive oil
- 1 lb. boneless, skinless chicken thighs
- ¼ tsp fine sea salt
- Ground black pepper
- 3 large carrots, peeled and thinly sliced
- 8 oz button mushrooms, sliced
- 1 small brown onion, sliced
- 1 cup Pinot Noir red wine
- 1 cup low-sodium chicken stock
- 1 tbsp. tomato paste
- 3 rosemary sprigs

1. Melt the butter in a large, heavy-bottom pan over medium-high heat. Sprinkle the chicken thighs with salt and pepper.
2. Once the butter starts to froth, add the chicken thighs, and brown for 1 to 2 minutes on each side. Transfer to a plate.
3. Add the carrots, mushrooms, and onion to the pan. Fry for 3 to 4 minutes, until the onion starts to soften. Add the red wine, chicken stock, tomato paste, and rosemary sprigs. Cook for 7 to 8 minutes, until the vegetables are tender.
4. Return the chicken thighs to the pan, and simmer for 5 to 10 minutes, until cooked through. Remove the rosemary sprigs and serve.

**PER SERVING**

Calories: 296; Total Fat: 12g; Saturated Fat: 3g; Cholesterol: 115mg; Sodium: 295mg; Total Carbs: 11g; Protein: 26g

## Turkey Oat Patties

**Prep time: 5 minutes | Cook time: 30 minutes | Serves 6**

- Aluminum foil
- 1 lb. lean ground turkey
- ½ cup rolled oats
- ¼ cup sun-dried tomatoes julienne cut, drained
- ¼ cup brown onion, finely chopped
- ¼ cup parsley, finely chopped
- 1 tbsp. garlic, crushed
- 6 whole-wheat hamburger buns
- 1 ripe avocado, peeled, pitted, and mashed
- 6 iceberg lettuce leaves
- 6 Roma tomato slices
- Hamburger dill pickle chips

1. Preheat the oven to broil. Line a baking sheet with aluminum foil.
2. In a large-sized mixing bowl, add the turkey, oats, sun-dried tomatoes, onion, parsley, and garlic, mix to combine. Shape into 6 patties.
3. Place the turkey patties on the baking sheet, and broil for 3 to 4 minutes on each side, until fully cooked and the juices run clear.
4. Meanwhile, prepare a self-serving platter with the buns, mashed avocado, lettuce leaves, tomato slices, and the dill pickle chips. Assemble the way you like.

**PER SERVING**

Calories: 366; Total Fat: 15g; Saturated Fat: 3g; Cholesterol: 52mg; Sodium: 353mg; Total Carbs: 35g; Protein: 24g.

# Chapter 7
# Meat

## Flank Steak with Caramelized Onions

**Prep time:10 minutes| Cook time:30 minutes| Serves 4**

- 2 large thinly sliced and halved lengthwise red onions,
- 1 tablespoon of butter
- 1/2 teaspoon of dried sage
- 1 green or red bell pepper; thin strips
- 11 -1/4 to 1 1/2 pounds, beef flank steak
- 1/2 teaspoon of dried oregano
- 1 tablespoon of black pepper; freshly ground.
- 1/2 teaspoon of salt
- 1 15-ounce can black beans rinsed and drained, warmed.
- 4 7- to 8-inch warmed flour tortillas

1. In a large pan over medium heat, melt the butter. Cover and simmer onions in it, occasionally turning, until they are soft, for approximately 7 minutes. Add sage, bell pepper strips, and oregano.
2. Cook, uncovered, over medium-high heat for 4 to 5 minutes, or until the peppers are crisp-tender and the onions are golden, stirring frequently. Preheat the grill pan to medium-high temperature.
3. Trim the fat off the steak and score it on both sides with shallow diamond cuts at 1-inch intervals. Season with salt and pepper. Grill, rotating once, for 8 to 12 minutes for the medium-rare or 12 to 15 minutes for the medium. Thinly slice steak across the grain diagonally and cover it with onion mixture. Warm the tortillas and black beans are served on the side.

**PER SERVING**

Calories: 434 kcal, Protein: 40 g, Carbohydrates: 36 g, Fat: 15 g, Cholesterol: 37 mg, Fiber: 3.4 g

## Juicy Burgers

**Prep time:10 minutes| Cook time:10 minutes| Serves 5**

- 1 cup low sodium beef broth
- 2 slices white bread, torn into pieces
- 1 1/2 pounds' extra-lean ground beef (93% lean)
- 2 tablespoons egg substitute
- 1/2 teaspoon black pepper

1. Microwave broth in a glass bowl for 30 seconds. Add bread pieces and combine with your hands.
2. Combine broth mixture and remaining ingredients. Shape into 5 patties. Grill patties over medium-high heat for 6 to 8 minutes on each side or to desired doneness.

**PER SERVING**

Calories: 328 kcal, Protein: 27 g, Carbohydrates: 0 g, Fat: 9 g, Cholesterol: 94 mg, Fiber: 0 g

## Steak and Vegetables with Chimichurri Sauce

**Prep time:20 minutes| Cook time:40 minutes| Serves 4**

- Steak & Vegetables
- ½ teaspoon of chili powder
- 1 pound of top sirloin beef steak; boneless, 1 inch thick
- ¼ teaspoon of salt
- 1 small red onion, 1/2-inch-thick slices
- 2 cups of cherry tomatoes or grape tomatoes
- Nonstick cooking spray
- 2 medium-trimmed zucchini or yellow summer squash halved lengthwise.

**CHIMICHURRI SAUCE**

- ½ cup of fresh cilantro; lightly packed
- 1 cup of fresh, lightly packed flat-leaf parsley
- ¼ cup of white wine vinegar
- 1 tablespoon of olive oil
- 2 tablespoons of water
- ¼ teaspoon of salt
- 6 minced cloves of garlic,
- ¼ teaspoon of crushed red pepper (Optional)
- ¼ teaspoon of ground black pepper

1. Trim the fat off the steak. Use a knife to cut the meat into four equal pieces. Season the steak pieces with 1/8 teaspoon of salt and chili powder. Using four 6- to 8-inch skewers, thread tomatoes onto the skewers. Lightly brush the zucchini, tomatoes, and red onion slices on both sides with nonstick spray. Sprinkle the remaining 1/8 tsp of salt into the veggies.
2. Place tomato skewers, steak, and vegetable slices on the uncovered grill rack directly over medium embers using a charcoal grill. Grill the steak until it reaches your preferred level of doneness, flipping once halfway through. Allow it 14 to 18 minutes for the medium-rare doneness (145 degrees Fahrenheit) or 18 to 22 minutes for the medium doneness (145 degrees Fahrenheit) to (160 degrees F). Grill onion slices and zucchini for 10 to 12 minutes, turning periodically, until soft and faintly browned in spots. Grill the tomatoes for 4 to 6 minutes, rotating once, or until softened and faintly browned. (Preheat the grill if using a gas grill.) Reduce to a medium heat setting. Place the tomato skewers, steak, and vegetable slices on the grill rack and cook them over high heat. Cover and cook as directed above).
3. Chimichurri Sauce Preparation: In a blender or food processor, combine cilantro, parsley, vinegar, olive oil, water, garlic, ground black pepper, salt, and, if preferred, crushed red pepper. Cover and mix or pulse several times on/off until chopped but not pureed. Using four serving dishes, divide the sliced meat. Grilled tomatoes, Chimichurri sauce, and veggie pieces are served on the side.

**PER SERVING**

Calories: 245 kcal, Protein: 28.3 g, Carbohydrates: 13.1 g, Fat: 8.6 g, Cholesterol: 47.6 mg, Fiber: 3.7 g

## Beef Noodle Soup

**Prep time:5 minutes| Cook time:25 minutes| Serves 4**

- 3 small baby bok choy; halved
- 1 tsp of oil
- 2 stalks of spring onions; diced
- 6 cups of beef broth; low sodium
- 2 tbsp. of soy sauce; reduced sodium
- 1/2 tsp of fresh ginger root; grated
- 2 1/2 cup of zucchini
- 1/4 cup of thai basil, shredded
- 1 1/4 lbs. lean beef; sliced
- 1/4 tsp of red pepper crushed flakes
- 1 tsp of sesame oil
- 1/4 tsp of black pepper

1. Cook the spring onions and Baby Bok Choy in a wok or pan with oil. Combine soy sauce, broth, and ginger in a large soup pot. Bring to a low simmer after covering it.
2. Add the steak strips to the soup after slicing it as thinly as possible. Simmer the soup to a moderate boil, then reduce to low heat, cover, and cook until the meat is fully cooked. Remove the soup from the heat and stir in the zucchini noodles. Add sesame oil, black pepper, basil, and crushed red pepper flakes. Serve hot with an equal quantity of soup in each dish.

**PER SERVING**

Calories: 361 kcal, Protein: 15.4 g, Carbohydrates: 32.1 g, Fat: 19 g, Cholesterol: 12.2 mg, Fiber: 4.4 g

## BBQ Pulled Pork with Greek Yogurt Slaw

**Prep time:10 minutes| Cook time:1 hour| Serves 4**

- 3 cups of green cabbage; shredded
- 1/2 cup of non-fat plain greek yogurt
- 3 cups of red cabbage; shredded
- 1 (12oz.) can of diet root beer
- 2 tsp of lemon juice
- 1 tbsp. of apple cider vinegar
- 1/4 tsp of celery salt
- 1 tsp of Dijon mustard
- 1 can of light cooking spray
- 1 1/2 lbs. pork tenderloin; halved
- 1 pinch stevia
- 4 sachets of buttermilk cheddar herb biscuit
- 1/2 cup of BBQ sauce; sugar-free

1. Cooking spray is used to coat the interior of the Instant Pot. On a high sauté ' setting, brown the pork chunks on all sides, approximately 3 minutes on each side.
2. Close the pressure valve after adding the diet root beer. Set the timer for 60 minutes on high. Allow for natural pressure release before opening. Prepare the slaw in the meanwhile. Combine cabbage, yogurt, apple cider vinegar, lemon juice, Dijon mustard, salt, and stevia in a medium-sized

mixing bowl.
3. Remove the pork from the Instant Pot and shred it in a bowl. Toss in the barbecue sauce and mix well. Bake Herb Biscuits according to package instructions, if desired. Serve the slaw and shredded pork on top of biscuits or without baked biscuits.

**PER SERVING**

Calories: 108 kcal, Protein: 5.8 g, Carbohydrates: 14 g, Fat: 2.5 g, Cholesterol: 39.9 mg, Fiber: 3.5 g

## Mexican Stuffed Peppers with Corn and Black Beans

**Prep time:10 minutes| Cook time:30 minutes| Serves 6**

- 6 bell peppers; any color
- 1 tablespoon of olive oil
- 1 chopped yellow onion,
- 2 minced cloves of garlic,
- 1 pound of lean ground beef
- 1 tablespoon of chili powder
- 1 1/2 teaspoons of ground cumin
- 1 (4-ounce) can diced green chiles
- 1 1/2 cups of cooked white rice
- 2 medium diced tomatoes,
- 1 (15-ounce) can have drained and rinsed black beans,
- 1 cup of defrosted frozen corn,
- 1/2 cup of shredded Cheddar cheese or Mexican-blend
- Optional toppings: Chopped fresh cilantro or green onions.

1. Preheat the oven to 350 degrees Fahrenheit. A big pot of water is brought to a boil. Slice the peppers in half vertically through the center of the stem and to the bottom. Remove the membranes as well as the seeds.
2. For 3–4 minutes, until the peppers are somewhat softened, parboil them in a saucepan of water. Drain the peppers and arrange them cut side up in a wide baking dish. Warm the oil in a wide skillet over medium heat. Sauté for 4 minutes, or until the onion is transparent. Cook for another minute after adding the garlic.
3. Cook for 5 minutes, or until the ground beef is brown, frequently stirring to break up the meat. Chili powder, green chiles, cooked rice, black beans, tomatoes, cumin, and maize are added. Season with pepper and salt to taste. Fill the peppers halfway with the ground beef rice mixture and top with cheese. Bake for 15-20 minutes, or until the peppers are soft and the cheese has melted. If using, garnish with cilantro or green onions and serve warm.

**PER SERVING**

Calories: 357 kcal, Protein: 26 g, Carbohydrates: 46 g, Fat: 7 g, Cholesterol: 46 mg, Fiber: 3 g

## Meatloaf

**Prep time:10 minutes| Cook time:1- 1 ½ hour| Serves 6**

- 1 1/2 pounds extra-lean ground beef (93% lean)
- 1 cup bread crumbs
- 1 onion, finely chopped
- 1/4 cup egg substitute
- 1/4 teaspoon black pepper
- 8 ounces no-salt-added tomato sauce, divided
- 1/2 cup water
- 2 teaspoons Worcestershire sauce
- 3 tablespoons vinegar
- 2 tablespoons mustard
- 3 tablespoons brown sugar

1. Preheat oven to 350°F (180°C, or gas mark 4). Mix beef, breadcrumbs, onion, egg substitute, pepper, and half the tomato sauce.
2. Form into one large loaf or two small ones; mix remaining tomato sauce and remaining ingredients together; pour over loaves. Bake for 1 to 1 1/2 hours.

**PER SERVING**

Calories: 393 kcal, Protein: 26 g, Carbohydrates: 23 g, Fat: 9 g, Cholesterol: 78 mg, Fiber: 1 g

## Oaxacan Tacos

**Prep time:10 minutes| Cook time:15 minutes| Serves 9**

- ground black pepper and salt to taste
- 2 pounds of top sirloin steak, thin strips
- 4 limes, wedges
- ¼ cup of vegetable oil
- 1 diced onion,
- 18 corn tortillas; (6 inches)
- 1 bunch of fresh cilantro; chopped,
- 4 fresh seeded and chopped jalapeno peppers

1. In a large skillet, heat the oil over medium-high heat. Put meat in the tit and cook for 5 minutes in a hot pan until the steak is browned on the outer side and is cooked through. Sprinkle salt & pepper to taste.
2. Place on a platter to keep warm. In the same skillet, heat the oil. Put the tortilla in the heated oil and cook until lightly browned and pliable, flipping once. Continue with the remaining tortillas. On a platter, arrange tortillas and top with steak, jalapeño, onion, and cilantro. Lime juice should be squeezed over the top.

**PER SERVING**

Calories: 379 kcal, Protein: 20.3 g, Carbohydrates: 28.1 g, Fat: 21.4 g, Cholesterol: 58.5 mg, Fiber: 1 g

## Beef and Broccoli Teriyaki Noodle Bowls

**Prep time:45 minutes| Cook time:20 minutes| Serves 4**

- 1 thinly sliced onion
- 1 1/4 teaspoon of dried ginger
- 4 ounces of thin rice noodles
- 1/4 cup of tamari sauce
- 3 cups of broccoli florets
- 1½ pound of skirt steak; thinly sliced against the grain.
- 1/4 teaspoon of red pepper flakes
- 3/4 cup of teriyaki sauce; gluten-free

1. Fill a large microwave-safe bowl halfway with water and microwave for 3 minutes, or until the water is extremely hot. Remove the water from the microwave and place noodles in the water. Allow 45 minutes for soaking.
2. Begin preparing the meat once the noodles have soaked for 30 minutes:
3. Over medium heat, sauté the cut onions and meat in a large pan. Cook until done, stirring often. Whisk the gluten-free teriyaki sauce, ginger, tamari sauce, and red pepper flakes in a small mixing bowl. Fill the skillet with the sauce. Stir everything together well. In the same skillet, add the broccoli.
4. Microwave the noodles for 2-3 minutes in water. Drain. Combine the meat, noodles, broccoli, and sauce in a pan. Toss to coat. Serve right away.

**PER SERVING**

Calories: 456 kcal, Protein: 44 g, Carbohydrates: 40 g, Fat: 13 g, Cholesterol: 85 mg, Fiber: 2 g

## Mexican Skillet Meal

**Prep time:5 minutes| Cook time:30 minutes| Serves 5**

- 1-pound extra-lean ground beef (93% lean)
- 1/2 cup onion, chopped
- 1/4 cup green bell peppers, chopped
- 1/4 cup red bell pepper, chopped
- 1/2 teaspoon minced garlic
- 3 cups water
- 2 teaspoons low sodium beef bouillon
- 2 cups canned no-salt-added tomatoes
- 1 tablespoon chili powder
- 1/2 teaspoon cumin
- 1/4 teaspoon dried oregano
- 1 2 ounces frozen corn, thawed

1. Sauté beef, onion, green and red bell peppers, and garlic in a large skillet until beef is browned and vegetables are tender.
2. Add rice and sauté 2 minutes longer. Stir in the remaining ingredients. Bring to boil. Reduce heat, cover, and simmer for 20 minutes, or until rice is tender and liquid is absorbed.

**PER SERVING**

Calories: 357 kcal, Protein: 22 g, Carbohydrates: 33 g, Fat: 7 g, Cholesterol: 63 mg, Fiber: 4 g

## Bistecca Alla Fiorentina Steak

**Prep time:1 hour 20 minutes | Cook time:20 minutes| Serves 6**

- 1 prime porterhouse steak (2- 1/2 pound)
- 4 sprigs of chopped fresh rosemary
- 3 tablespoons of Tuscan olive oil
- 6 lemon wedges
- Grey moist, pepper, and sea salt to taste, freshly cracked.

1. This dish is also known as Tuscan Peter house steak.
2. Hardwood charcoal can be used to start an outdoor grill. Spread chopped rosemary on all sides of steak, place on a platter, and leave aside to marinate for 1 hour at room temperature. Arrange for maximum heat when the coals are white and blazing.
3. Brush or massage olive oil over the steak, then season with sea salt & pepper to taste. Place steak on the grill and cook for 5 to 10 mins, depending on the thickness of the meat, until dark golden brown (not burned) crust develops. Cook for another 5 to 10 mins, or until golden brown on the opposite side. Place the steak on a plate and set it aside to sit for 10 mins.
4. Remove the 2 pieces off the bone and put them on the serving plate. Trim any excess fat from round steak (tenderloin) before slicing it into 6 equal pieces and fanning them out on one side of the bone. Slice the rectangular steak (loin) into 1/4-inch pieces at an angle to the grain. On the other side of the bone, fan out. Finish with lemon wedges and a sprinkling of sea salt on top of the dish.

**PER SERVING**

Calories: 346 kcal, Protein: 18.2 g, Carbohydrates: 1.5 g, Fat: 29.6 g, Cholesterol: 62.8 mg, Fiber: 3 g

## London Broil

**Prep time:5 minutes | Cook time:15 minutes| Serves 5**

1/4 cup olive oil
1 teaspoon cider vinegar
1/4 teaspoon minced garlic
1/4 teaspoon freshly ground black pepper
1 1/2 pounds beef round steak

1. Score steak on both sides. Combine oil, vinegar, garlic, and pepper in a resalable plastic bag. Add steak and marinate for several hours, turning occasionally. Preheat broiler.
2. Remove steak from marinade and broil 3 inches (7.5 cm) from heat for 4 to 5 minutes. Turn and broil 4 to 5 minutes longer, or until medium-rare. Carve in thin slices against the grain.

**PER SERVING**

Calories: 367 kcal, Protein: 49 g, Carbohydrates: 0 g, Fat: 18 g, Cholesterol: 122 mg, Fiber: 0 g

## Tailgate Chili

**Prep time:5 minutes | Cook time:35 minutes | Serves 4**

- 1 medium chopped onion
- 1 lb. ground beef; 95% lean
- 1 medium chopped jalapeño
- 1 medium green chopped bell pepper
- 1 Tbsp. of chili powder
- 4 cloves of fresh garlic; minced, OR 2 tsp. of jarred minced garlic.
- 1/2 tsp. of ground coriander
- 1 Tbsp. of ground cumin
- 15.5 oz. canned, low-sodium, or no-salt-added pinto/kidney beans, rinsed and drained.
- 3/4 cup of jarred salsa (low sodium)
- 14.5 oz. of canned, low-sodium or no-salt-added, diced tomatoes (undrained)

1. Use a cooking spray to coat a big pot. Add and cook beef for 5-7 minutes over medium-high heat, frequently stirring to break up the meat. Drain excess fat in a strainer by rinsing with water.
2. Return the meat into the pot. Cook for 5 minutes, stirring periodically, after adding the chili powder, garlic, bell pepper, and cumin. Bring the remaining ingredients to a boil.
3. Reduce the heat to a low, cover, and cook for 20 minutes. If desired, serve with fat-free sour cream, low-fat grated cheese, sliced avocado, chopped green onions, or trimmed cilantro.

**PER SERVING**

Calories: 297 kcal, Protein: 31 g, Carbohydrates: 29 g, Fat: 6 g, Cholesterol: 62 mg, Fiber: 7 g

## Mojo Flat Iron Steak

**Prep time:40 minutes | Cook time:20 minutes| Serves 4**

- 1 teaspoon of chili powder
- 2 teaspoons of brown sugar
- 1 (1-pound) trimmed flat iron steak
- ¼ cup of fresh orange juice
- 2 teaspoons of grated orange rind
- ¼ teaspoon of chipotle chile powder; ground
- 2 minced garlic cloves,
- 1 teaspoon of kosher salt; divided.
- Cooking spray
- 2 teaspoons of grated lime rind
- 1 cup of peeled, seeded cucumber; finely chopped.
- 2 tablespoons of olive oil; extra-virgin, divided.
- 3 tablespoons of fresh lime juice, divided.
- 1 cup of red bell pepper; finely chopped.
- 3 tablespoons of red onion; finely chopped.
- ¼ cup of fresh orange juice
- 1 seeded and finely chopped jalapeño pepper
- 2 tablespoons of chopped fresh cilantro.

1. In a mixing bowl, whisk the orange juice, orange rind, lime rind, 1 tablespoon oil, 2 tablespoons lime juice, cloves, brown sugar, chili powder, and chipotle chile powder. Add the steak and turn to cover it with the sauce. Allow it to sit at room temperature for 30 minutes, rotating periodically.
2. Preheat a grill pan to high. Spray the pan with nonstick cooking spray. Remove the meat from the marinade and discard the marinade. Using 1/2 teaspoon of salt, season the meat. Add the steak to the pan and cook it for 5 minutes on each side for medium-rare or until desired doneness is reached. Place the steak on a chopping board and let it rest for 5 minutes. Using a sharp knife, cut steak across the grain. In a mixing dish, combine the remaining 1 tablespoon oil, 1/2 teaspoon salt, 1 tablespoon of lime juice, and the other ingredients. Serve alongside a steak.

**PER SERVING**

Calories: 216 kcal, Protein: 24 g, Carbohydrates: 6 g, Fat: 11.1 g, Cholesterol: 81 mg, Fiber: 1 g

## Beef Fajita

**Prep time:10 minutes | Cook time:15-20 minutes| Serves 4**

- ¼ red pepper; thinly sliced.
- 1 corn tortilla
- ¼ red onion; thinly sliced.
- 60 g beef; cut it into pieces.
- ¼ green pepper; thinly sliced.
- 1 tsp of plain yogurt
- 1 tbsp of cilantro; chopped.
- ½ tsp of olive oil
- ¼ tsp of chili powder

1. Heat the oil in a skillet before adding the onion and peppers. After adding the beef, cook for another 3 minutes or until beef is cooked through.
2. Combine the chili powder and yogurt in a small bowl and distribute them over the tortilla. Place all cooked items on the tortilla, along with the cilantro, and serve.

**PER SERVING**

Calories: 225 kcal, Protein: 14.2 g, Carbohydrates: 12.9 g, Fat: 11 g, Cholesterol: 35 mg, Fiber: 2.9 g.

# Chapter 8
# Fish and Seafood

## Roasted Shrimp and Veggies
**Prep time:10 minutes | Cook time: 20 minutes| Serves 4**

- 1 cup sliced cremini mushrooms
- 2 medium chopped Yukon Gold potatoes, rinsed, unpeeled
- 2 cups broccoli florets
- 3 cloves garlic, sliced
- 1 cup sliced fresh green beans
- 1 cup cauliflower florets
- 2 tablespoons fresh lemon juice
- 2 tablespoons low-sodium vegetable broth
- 1 teaspoon olive oil
- 1 teaspoon dried thyme
- ½ teaspoon dried oregano
- Pinch salt
- ⅛ teaspoon black pepper
- ½ pound medium shrimp, peeled and deveined

1. Preheat the oven to 400°F.
2. In a large baking pan, combine the mushrooms, potatoes, broccoli, garlic, green beans, and cauliflower, and toss to coat.
3. In a small bowl, combine the lemon juice, broth, olive oil, thyme, oregano, salt, and pepper and mix well. Drizzle over the vegetables
4. Roast for 15 minutes, then stir.
5. Add the shrimp and distribute evenly.
6. Roast for another 5 minutes or until the shrimp curl and turn pink. Serve immediately.

**PER SERVING**

Calories 192; Fat 3g (with 14% calories from fat); Saturated fat 0g; Monounsaturated fat 1g; Carbs 29g; Sodium 116mg; Dietary fiber 5g; Protein 17g; Cholesterol 86mg; Vitamin A 12% DV; Vitamin C 138% DV; Sugar 3g

## Shrimp and Pineapple Lettuce Wraps
**Prep time:15 minutes | Cook time: 12 minutes| Serves 4**

- 2 teaspoons olive oil
- 2 jalapeño peppers, seeded and minced
- 6 scallions, chopped
- 2 yellow bell peppers, seeded and chopped
- 8 ounces small shrimp, peeled and deveined
- 2 cups canned pineapple chunks, drained, reserving juice
- 2 tablespoons fresh lime juice
- 1 avocado, peeled, and cubed
- 1 large carrot, coarsely grated
- 8 romaine or Boston lettuce leaves, rinsed and dried

1. In a medium saucepan, heat the olive oil over medium heat.
2. Add the jalapeño pepper and scallions and cook for 2 minutes, stirring constantly.
3. Add the bell pepper, and cook for 2 minutes.
4. Add the shrimp, and cook for 1 minute, stirring constantly.
5. Add the pineapple, 2 tablespoons of the reserved pineapple juice, and lime juice, and bring to a simmer. Simmer for 1 minute longer or until the shrimp curl and turn pink. Let the mixture cool for 5 minutes.
6. Serve the shrimp mixture with the cubed avocado and grated carrot, wrapped in the lettuce leaves.

**PER SERVING**

Calories 241; Fat 9g (with 33% calories from fat); Saturated fat 2g; Monounsaturated fat 5g; Carbs 29g; Sodium 109mg; Dietary fiber 6g; Protein 6g; Cholesterol 109mg; Vitamin A 96% DV; Vitamin C 332% DV; Sugar 16g

## Grilled Scallops with Gremolata
**Prep time:15 minutes | Cook time: 6 minutes| Serves 4**

- 2 scallions, cut into pieces
- ¾ cup packed fresh flat-leaf parsley
- ¼ cup packed fresh basil leaves
- 1 teaspoon lemon zest
- 3 tablespoons fresh lemon juice
- 1 tablespoon olive oil
- 20 sea scallops
- 2 teaspoons butter, melted
- Pinch salt
- ⅛ teaspoon lemon pepper

1. Prepare and preheat the grill to medium-high. Make sure the grill rack is clean.
2. Meanwhile, make the gremolata. In a blender or food processor, combine the scallions, parsley, basil, lemon zest, lemon juice, and olive oil. Blend or process until the herbs are finely chopped. Pour into a small bowl and set aside.
3. Put the scallops on a plate. If the scallops have a small tough muscle attached to them, remove and discard it. Brush the melted butter over the scallops. Sprinkle with the salt and the lemon pepper.
4. Place the scallops in a grill basket, if you have one. If not, place a sheet of heavy-duty foil on the grill, punch some holes in it, and arrange the scallops evenly across it.
5. Grill the scallops for 2 to 3 minutes per side, turning once, until opaque. Drizzle with the gremolata and serve.

**PER SERVING**

Calories 190; Fat 7g (with 33% calories from fat); Saturated fat 2g; Monounsaturated fat 3g; Carbs 2g; Sodium 336mg; Dietary fiber 1g; Protein 28g; Cholesterol 68mg; Vitamin A 27% DV; Vitamin C 37% DV; Sugar 1g

## Healthy Paella

**Prep time:15 minutes | Cook time: 15 minutes | Serves 4**

- 1 tablespoon olive oil
- 1 onion, chopped
- 3 cloves garlic, minced
- 1 red bell pepper, seeded and chopped
- 2½ cups low-sodium vegetable broth
- 1 tomato, chopped
- 1 teaspoon smoked paprika
- 1 teaspoon dried thyme leaves
- ¼ teaspoon turmeric
- ⅛ teaspoon black pepper
- 1 cup whole-wheat orzo
- ½ pound halibut fillets, cut into 1-inch pieces
- 12 medium shrimp, peeled and deveined
- ¼ cup chopped fresh flat-leaf parsley

1. In a large deep skillet, heat the olive oil over medium heat.
2. Add the onion, garlic, and red bell pepper, and cook, stirring, for 2 minutes.
3. Add the vegetable broth, tomato, paprika, thyme, turmeric, and black pepper, and bring to a simmer.
4. Stir in the orzo, making sure it is submerged in the liquid in the pan. Simmer for 5 minutes, stirring occasionally.
5. Add the halibut and stir. Simmer for 4 minutes.
6. Add the shrimp and stir. Simmer for 2 to 3 minutes or until the shrimp curl and turn pink and the pasta is cooked al dente.
7. Sprinkle with the parsley, and serve immediately.

### PER SERVING

Calories 367; Fat 7g (with 17% calories from fat); Saturated fat 1g; Monounsaturated fat 3g; Carbs 50g; Sodium 147mg; Dietary fiber 9g; Protein 25g; Cholesterol 50mg; Vitamin A 38% DV; Vitamin C 84% DV; Sugar 5g

## Vietnamese Fish and Noodle Bowl

**Prep time: 15 minutes | Cook time: 15 minutes | Serves 3**

- ¾ pound grouper fillets, cut into 1-inch pieces
- 1 tablespoon corn starch
- ⅛ teaspoon cayenne pepper
- 2 teaspoons fish sauce
- 1 tablespoon rice wine vinegar
- 1 teaspoon sugar
- 2 tablespoons fresh lemon juice
- 1 teaspoon olive oil
- ¼ cup minced daikon radish
- 3 cloves garlic, minced
- 4 ounces whole-wheat spaghetti, broken in half
- 1½ cups low-sodium vegetable broth
- 2 tablespoons chopped peanuts
- 2 tablespoons minced fresh cilantro
- 2 tablespoons minced fresh basil

1. In a medium bowl, toss the grouper with the cornstarch and cayenne pepper and set aside.
2. In a small bowl, combine the fish sauce, rice wine vinegar, sugar, and lemon juice, and stir to mix well.
3. In a large skillet, heat the olive oil over medium heat. Add the daikon and garlic and cook for 1 minute, stirring constantly.
4. Add the fish to the skillet; sauté for 2 to 3 minutes, stirring frequently, until the fish browns lightly.
5. Remove the fish mixture to a large bowl and set aside.
6. Add the spaghetti and vegetable broth to the skillet, and stir. Bring to a simmer over high heat and cook for 7 to 8 minutes or until the pasta is al dente.
7. Return the fish and radish mixture to the skillet along with the fish sauce mixture, peanuts, cilantro, and basil. Toss for 1 minute, then serve immediately in bowls.

### PER SERVING

Calories 324; Fat 6g (with 17% calories from fat); Saturated fat 1g; Monounsaturated fat 3g; Carbs 38g; Sodium 439mg; Dietary fiber 1g; Protein 30g; Cholesterol 46mg; Vitamin A 7% DV; Vitamin C 12% DV; Sugar 3g

## Cod Satay

Prep time:15 minutes | Cook time: 15 minutes| Serves 4

- 2 teaspoons olive oil, divided
- 1 small onion, diced
- 2 cloves garlic, minced
- ⅓ cup low-fat coconut milk
- 1 tomato, chopped
- 2 tablespoons low-fat peanut butter
- 1 tablespoon packed brown sugar
- ⅓ cup low-sodium vegetable broth
- 2 teaspoons low-sodium soy sauce
- ⅛ teaspoon ground ginger
- Pinch red pepper flakes
- 4 (6-ounce) cod fillets
- ⅛ teaspoon white pepper

1. In a small saucepan, heat 1 teaspoon of the olive oil over medium heat.
2. Add the onion and garlic, and cook, stirring frequently for 3 minutes.
3. Add the coconut milk, tomato, peanut butter, brown sugar, broth, soy sauce, ginger, and red pepper flakes, and bring to a simmer, stirring with a whisk until the sauce combines. Simmer for 2 minutes, then remove the satay sauce from the heat and set aside.
4. Season the cod with the white pepper.
5. Heat a large nonstick skillet with the remaining 1 teaspoon olive oil, and add the cod fillets. Cook for 3 minutes, then turn and cook for 3 to 4 minutes more or until the fish flakes when tested with a fork.
6. Cover the fish with the satay sauce and serve immediately.

**PER SERVING**

Calories 255; Fat 10g (with 35% calories from fat); Saturated fat 5g; Monounsaturated fat 3g; Carbs 9g; Sodium 222mg; Dietary fiber 1g; Protein 33g; Cholesterol 72mg; Vitamin A 4% DV; Vitamin C 9% DV; Sugar 4g

## Crispy Mixed Nut Fish Fillets

Prep time:10 minutes | Cook time: 15 minutes| Serves 4

- 4 (6-ounce) white fish fillets, such as red snapper or cod
- 2 tablespoons low-sodium yellow mustard
- 2 tablespoons nonfat plain Greek yogurt
- 2 tablespoons low-fat buttermilk
- 1 teaspoon dried Italian herb seasoning
- ⅛ teaspoon white pepper
- ¼ cup hazelnut flour
- 2 tablespoons almond flour
- 2 tablespoons ground almonds
- 2 tablespoons ground hazelnuts

1. Preheat the oven to 400°F. Line a baking sheet with a fine wire rack and set aside.
2. Pat the fish dry and place on a plate.
3. In a shallow bowl, combine the mustard, yogurt, buttermilk, Italian seasoning, and white pepper.
4. On a plate, combine the hazelnut flour and almond flour, and add the ground almonds, the ground hazelnuts, and mix well.
5. Coat the fish with the mustard mixture, then coat with the nut mixture. Place on the prepared baking sheet.
6. Bake the fish for 12 to 17 minutes, until it flakes when tested with a fork. Serve immediately.

**PER SERVING**

Calories 256; Fat 9g (with 32% calories from fat); Saturated fat 1g; Monounsaturated fat 5g; Carbs 4g; Sodium 206mg; Dietary fiber 2g; Protein 38g; Cholesterol 63mg; Vitamin A 4% DV; Vitamin C 6% DV; Sugar 2g

## Steamed Sole Rolls with Greens

Prep time:15 minutes | Cook time: 10 minutes| Serves 4

- 4 (6-ounce) sole fillets
- 2 teaspoons grated peeled fresh ginger root
- 2 cloves garlic, minced
- 2 teaspoons low-sodium soy sauce
- 1 tablespoon rice wine vinegar
- 1 teaspoon toasted sesame oil
- 2 cups fresh torn spinach leaves
- 1 cup fresh stemmed torn kale
- 1 cup sliced mushrooms
- 2 teaspoons toasted sesame seeds

1. Cut the sole fillets in half lengthwise. Sprinkle each piece with some of the ginger root and garlic. Roll up the fillets, ginger root side in. Fasten with a toothpick and set aside.
2. In a small bowl, combine the soy sauce, vinegar, and toasted sesame oil.
3. Bring water to a boil over medium heat in a large shallow saucepan that will hold your steamer.
4. Arrange the spinach leaves and kale in the bottom of the steamer. Add the rolled sole fillets. Add the mushrooms, and sprinkle everything with the soy sauce mixture.
5. Cover and steam for 7 to 11 minutes or until the fish is cooked and flakes when tested with a fork. Remove the toothpicks.
6. To serve, sprinkle with the sesame seeds and serve the fish on top of the wilted greens and mushrooms.

**PER SERVING**

Calories 263; Fat 8g (with 27% calories from fat); Saturated fat 2g; Monounsaturated fat 3g; Carbs 7g; Sodium 247mg; Dietary fiber 3g; Protein 36g; Cholesterol 81mg; Vitamin A 81% DV; Vitamin C 47% DV; Sugar 0g

## Red Snapper Scampi

**Prep time:10 minutes | Cook time: 20 minutes| Serves 4**

- 2 teaspoons olive oil
- 4 cloves garlic, minced
- ¼ cup fresh lemon juice
- ¼ cup white wine or fish stock
- 1 teaspoon fresh lemon zest
- Pinch salt
- ⅛ teaspoon lemon pepper
- 4 (6-ounce) red snapper fillets
- 2 scallions, minced
- 3 tablespoons minced flat-leaf fresh parsley

1. Preheat the oven to 400°F. Line a baking pan with parchment paper.
2. In a small bowl, combine the olive oil, garlic, lemon juice, white wine, lemon zest, salt, and lemon pepper.
3. Arrange the fillets skin side down, if the skin is attached, on the prepared baking pan. Pour the lemon juice mixture over the fillets.
4. Roast for 15 to 20 minutes, or until the fish flakes when tested with a fork.
5. Serve the fish with the pan drippings, sprinkled with the scallions and parsley.

**PER SERVING**

Calories 212; Fat 5g (with 21% calories from fat); Saturated fat 1g; Monounsaturated fat 2g; Carbs 3g; Sodium 112mg; Dietary fiber 0g; Protein 35g; Cholesterol 62mg; Vitamin A 10% DV; Vitamin C 26% DV; Sugar 1g

## Orange Thyme Red Snapper

**Prep time:5 minutes | Cook time: 10 minutes| Serves 4**

- 1 medium orange
- 2 teaspoons olive oil
- 4 (6-ounce) fillets red snapper
- Pinch salt
- ⅛ teaspoon white pepper
- 2 teaspoons olive oil
- 2 scallions, chopped
- 1½ teaspoons fresh thyme leaves, or ½ teaspoon dried

1. Rinse the orange and dry. Using a small grater or zester, remove 1 teaspoon zest from the orange and set aside. Cut the orange in half, squeeze in a small bowl, and reserve the juice.
2. Add the olive oil to a large nonstick skillet and place over medium heat. Meanwhile, sprinkle the fish with the salt and white pepper.
3. Add the fish to the skillet, skin-side down, if the skin is attached. Cook 3 minutes on one side, briefly pressing on the fish with a spatula to prevent curling (or slit the fillet to prevent curling). Turn the fish and cook for 2 to 3 minutes on the second side, until the fish flakes when tested with a fork.
4. Transfer the fish to a plate. Remove the skin, if present, and discard. Cover the fish with a foil tent to keep it warm.
5. Add the scallions and the thyme to the skillet; cook and stir gently for 1 minute. Add the reserved orange juice and orange zest and simmer for 2 to 3 minutes or until the liquid is slightly reduced.
6. Pour the sauce over the fish and serve immediately.

**PER SERVING**

Calories 232; Fat 7g (with 27% calories from fat); Saturated fat 1g; Monounsaturated fat 4g; Carbs 6g; Sodium 121mg; Dietary fiber 1g; Protein 35g; Cholesterol 62mg; Vitamin A 7% DV; Vitamin C 48% DV; Sugar 5g

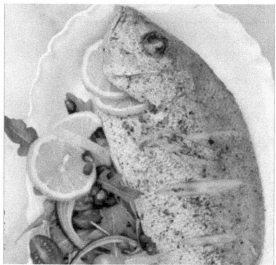

## Catalán Salmon Tacos

**Prep time:10 minutes | Cook time: 20 minutes| Serves 4**

- 1 teaspoon olive oil
- 1 (6-ounce) salmon fillet
- 1 teaspoon chili powder
- ½ teaspoon dried oregano leaves
- ⅛ teaspoon black pepper
- 1 small onion, diced
- 2 cloves peeled garlic, minced
- 1 (16-ounce) can low-sodium white beans, rinsed and drained
- 1 tomato, chopped
- 1 cup torn fresh Swiss chard leaves
- 2 tablespoons pine nuts
- 4 corn tortillas, heated

1. Add the olive oil to a large nonstick skillet and place over medium heat. Rub the salmon fillet with the chili powder, oregano, and pepper.
2. Add the salmon to the pan, skin side down. Cook for 3 minutes, then turn and cook for 5 minutes longer, or until the fish flakes when tested with a fork. Remove the salmon from the pan, flake, and set aside.
3. Add the onion and garlic to the pan and cook for 2 to 3 minutes, stirring frequently, until softened.
4. Add the beans and mash some of them into the onions. Cook for 1 minute, stirring occasionally.
5. Add the tomato and Swiss chard and cook for another 1 to 2 minutes until the greens start to wilt. Add the pine nuts to the mixture.
6. Make the tacos by adding the bean mixture and the salmon to the corn tortillas, and fold them in half. Serve immediately.

**PER SERVING**

Calories 296; Fat 8g (with 24% calories from fat); Saturated fat 1g; Monounsaturated fat 3g; Carbs 39g; Sodium 63mg; Dietary fiber 8g; Protein 19g; Cholesterol 23mg; Vitamin A 20% DV; Vitamin C 15% DV; Sugar 2g

## Salmon with Farro Pilaf

**Prep time:5 minutes | Cook time: 25 minutes| Serves 4**

- ½ cup farro
- 1¼ cups low-sodium vegetable broth
- 4 (4-ounce) salmon fillets
- Pinch salt
- ½ teaspoon dried marjoram leaves
- ⅛ teaspoon white pepper
- ¼ cup dried cherries
- ¼ cup dried currants
- 1 cup fresh baby spinach leaves
- 1 tablespoon orange juice

1. Preheat the oven to 400°F. Line a baking sheet with parchment paper and set aside.
2. In a medium saucepan over medium heat, combine the farro and the vegetable broth and bring to a simmer. Reduce the heat to low and simmer, partially covered, for 25 minutes, or until the farro is tender.
3. Meanwhile, sprinkle the salmon with the salt, marjoram, and white pepper and place on the prepared baking sheet.
4. When the farro has cooked for 10 minutes, bake the salmon in the oven for 12 to 15 minutes, or until the salmon flakes when tested with a fork. Remove and cover to keep warm.
5. When the farro is tender, add the cherries, currants, spinach, and orange juice; stir and cover. Let stand off the heat for 2 to 3 minutes.
6. Plate the salmon and serve with the farro pilaf.

**PER SERVING**

Calories 304; Fat 8g (with 24% calories from fat); Saturated fat 1g; Monounsaturated fat 2g; Carbs 32g; Sodium 139mg; Dietary fiber 3g; Protein 26g; Cholesterol 62mg; Vitamin A 12% DV; Vitamin C 2% DV; Sugar 17g

## Maple-Garlic Salmon and Cauliflower Sheet Pan Dinner

**Prep time: 5 minutes, plus 30 minutes to marinate | Cook time: 20 minutes | Serves 4**

- 1 pound salmon fillet
- 3 tablespoons minced garlic, divided
- 2 tablespoons olive oil, divided
- 2 tablespoons low-sodium soy sauce
- Freshly ground black pepper
- 2½ cups bite-size cauliflower florets
- Pinch sea salt
- 1½ tablespoons maple syrup

1. Place the salmon, 2 tablespoons garlic, 1 tablespoon oil, soy sauce, and pepper in a resealable plastic bag and place the bag in the refrigerator. Let the fish marinate for 30 minutes or overnight.
2. Preheat the oven to 425°F. Line a baking sheet with parchment paper.
3. In a medium bowl, toss the cauliflower with the remaining olive oil, garlic, more pepper, and a pinch of salt, and place it on half of the prepared baking sheet.
4. Place the marinated salmon on the other half of the sheet and bake for 20 minutes until the fish is slightly golden brown on the edges and just cooked through. Transfer the fish from the baking sheet to a plate and loosely cover it with foil to keep it warm. Flip the cauliflower and bake for 10 minutes more, until soft.
5. Drizzle the maple syrup over the salmon and serve with the cauliflower.

**PER SERVING (3 OUNCES OF FISH AND ½ CUP CAULIFLOWER)**

Calories: 216; Total fat: 11g; Saturated fat: 2g; Trans fat: 0g; Protein: 20g; Total carbohydrate: 9g; Fiber: 1g; Sodium: 293mg; Potassium: 658mg

## Spicy Trout Sheet Pan Dinner

**Prep time: 5 minutes | Cook time: 20 minutes | Serves 4**

- 3 tablespoons minced garlic, divided
- 2 tablespoons chili powder, divided
- 2 tablespoons olive oil, divided
- Sea salt
- 1 pound rainbow trout fillets
- 2 zucchini, sliced into rounds

1. Preheat the oven to 425°F. Line a baking sheet with parchment paper.
2. In a medium bowl, mix 2 tablespoons of garlic, 1 tablespoon of chili powder, 1 tablespoon of olive oil, and a pinch of salt. Generously coat both sides of the trout fillets with the garlic mixture and place them on one half of the baking sheet.
3. In another medium bowl, mix the remaining garlic, chili powder, olive oil, and another pinch of salt. Add the zucchini to the bowl and stir to combine.
4. Bake the fish for 20 minutes until slightly browned on the edges. Add the zucchini to the empty side of the baking sheet halfway through the cooking time. Enjoy immediately.

**PER SERVING (3 OUNCES OF TROUT AND ½ CUP ZUCCHINI)**

Calories: 186; Total fat: 9g; Saturated fat: 2g; Trans fat: 0g; Protein: 20g; Total carbohydrate: 6g; Fiber: 2g; Sodium: 158mg; Potassium: 724mg

## Salmon Patties

**Prep time: 20 minutes | Cook time: 40 minutes | Serves 4**

- ¼ cup quinoa, rinsed
- ½ cup water
- 2 (7½-ounce) cans low-sodium deboned salmon, packed in water
- 1 tablespoon mustard
- 1 teaspoon Old Bay Seasoning
- 2 large eggs
- olive oil

1. In a medium saucepan over high heat, combine the quinoa and water and bring to a boil. Reduce the heat to low, and simmer until the liquid is absorbed, about 20 minutes. Remove from the heat, fluff with a fork, and let cool.
2. In a large bowl, mix the salmon, mustard, and seasoning until well combined.
3. Add the quinoa and eggs and combine well, then shape the mixture into 5 patties.
4. Place the patties on the prepared baking sheet and bake for 20 minutes, until they are slightly brown on the edges. Serve hot.

**PER SERVING (1 PATTY)**

Calories: 202; Total fat: 10g; Saturated fat: 2g; Trans fat: 0g; Protein: 23g; Total carbohydrate: 6g; Fiber: 1g; Sodium: 480mg; Potassium: 310mg

## Salmon with Spicy Mixed Beans

**Prep time:5 minutes | Cook time: 20 minutes| Serves 4**

- 2 teaspoons olive oil, divided
- 4 (4-ounce) salmon fillets
- Pinch salt
- ⅛ teaspoon black pepper
- 1 onion, diced
- 3 cloves peeled garlic, minced
- 1 jalapeño pepper, seeded and minced
- 1 (16-ounce) can low-sodium mixed beans, rinsed and drained
- 2 tablespoons low-fat plain Greek yogurt
- 2 tablespoons minced fresh cilantro

1. Put 1 teaspoon of the olive oil in a large skillet and heat over medium heat.
2. Sprinkle the salmon fillets with the salt and pepper and add to the skillet, skin side down.
3. Cook for 5 minutes, then flip the fillets with a spatula and cook for another 3 to 4 minutes or until the salmon flakes when tested with a fork. Remove the fish to a clean warm plate, and cover with an aluminum foil tent to keep warm.
4. Add the remaining 1 teaspoon of the olive oil to the skillet. Add the onion, garlic, and jalapeño pepper; cook, stirring frequently, for 3 minutes.
5. Add the beans and mash with a fork until desired consistency.
6. Remove the pan from the heat, add the yogurt, and stir until combined.
7. Pile the beans onto a serving platter, top with the fish, and sprinkle with the cilantro. Serve immediately.

**PER SERVING**

Calories 293; Fat 10g (with 30% calories from fat); Saturated fat 2g; Monounsaturated fat 4g; Carbs 23g; Sodium 345mg; Dietary fiber 7g; Protein 29g; Cholesterol 62mg; Vitamin A 2% DV; Vitamin C 10% DV; Sugar 4g

## Arctic Char with Tomato Pear Compote

**Prep time:5 minutes | Cook time: 25 minutes| Serves 4**

- 1 scallion, minced
- 1 pint cherry tomatoes
- 1 ripe pear, cored and chopped
- 1 teaspoon olive oil
- 2 tablespoons fresh lemon juice
- 1 tablespoon honey
- 4 (4-ounce) arctic char fillets
- Pinch salt
- ⅛ teaspoon white pepper
- 2 tablespoons chopped fresh mint

1. Preheat the oven to 400°F. Line a baking sheet with parchment paper.
2. Combine the scallion, cherry tomatoes, and pear on the prepared baking sheet and toss to mix. Drizzle with the olive oil, lemon juice, and honey, and toss again.
3. Roast for 10 minutes, then remove and stir. Make room for the fish fillets on the pan.
4. Place the fish fillets skin side down in the pan. Return the pan to the oven and roast for 12 to 15 minutes or until the cherry tomatoes are soft with brown spots and the fish flakes when tested with a fork.
5. Remove the pan from the oven. Use a spatula to lift the fish fillets off the skin and place on a warmed serving platter.
6. Toss the roasted fruits with the mint and serve with the fish.

**PER SERVING**

Calories 228; Fat 8g (with 32% calories from fat); Saturated fat 1g; Monounsaturated fat 3g; Carbs 15g; Sodium 54mg; Dietary fiber 2g; Protein 24g; Cholesterol 62mg; Vitamin A 14% DV; Vitamin C 25% DV; Sugar 11g

## Mediterranean Roasted Mahi Mahi with Broccoli

**Prep time:5 minutes | Cook time: 22 minutes| Serves 4**

- 2 cups broccoli florets
- 2 tablespoons olive oil, divided
- 4 (6-ounce) mahi mahi fillets
- 1 cup cherry tomatoes
- 2 cloves peeled garlic, sliced
- ⅛ teaspoon white pepper
- 1 teaspoon paprika
- 2 tablespoons fresh lemon juice
- 2 tablespoons crumbled feta cheese

1. Preheat the oven to 400°F. Line a baking sheet with parchment paper.
2. Place the broccoli florets on the prepared baking sheet. Drizzle with 1 tablespoon of the olive oil and toss to coat. Spread the broccoli in a single layer.
3. Roast the broccoli for 10 minutes.
4. Remove the baking sheet from the oven. Move the broccoli over to make room for the fish. Place the fish, cherry tomatoes, and garlic on the baking sheet. Sprinkle the fish with the white pepper and paprika.
5. In a small bowl, combine the lemon juice and the remaining 1 tablespoon olive oil, and drizzle over the fish and vegetable mixture.
6. Roast for 10 to 12 minutes longer, or until the fish flakes when tested with a fork and the broccoli is tender.
7. Sprinkle with the feta cheese and serve immediately.

**PER SERVING**

Calories 258; Fat 11g (with 38% calories from fat); Saturated fat 2g; Monounsaturated fat 6g; Carbs 6g; Sodium 171mg; Dietary fiber 2g; Protein 33g; Cholesterol 72mg; Vitamin A 18% DV; Vitamin C 82% DV; Sugar 2g.

# Chapter 9
# Vegetarian

## Roasted Root Veggies and Spiced Lentils

**Prep time:5 minutes| Cook time:45 minutes| Serves 4**

### LENTILS

- ½ cup of French green lentils or black beluga lentils
- 1 ½ cups of water
- ½ teaspoon of ground coriander
- 1 teaspoon of garlic powder
- ¼ teaspoon of ground allspice
- ½ teaspoon of ground cumin
- ¼ teaspoon of kosher salt
- 1 teaspoon of olive oil; extra-virgin
- 2 tablespoons of lemon juice

### VEGETABLES

- 1 1/2 cups of roasted root vegetables
- 1 smashed clove of garlic,
- 2 cups of chopped beet greens or kale
- ⅛ teaspoon of ground pepper
- 1 teaspoon of ground coriander
- 1 tablespoon of olive oil; extra-virgin
- dash of kosher salt
- For garnish; fresh parsley
- 2 tablespoons of plain low-fat yogurt or tahini

1. To make lentils: In a medium saucepan, mix the lentils, water, garlic powder, cumin, 1/4 teaspoon of salt, allspice, 1/2 teaspoon of coriander, and sumac (if using). Boil it. Reduce heat to keep the simmer, cover, and cook for 25 to 30 minutes. Uncover and continue to cook for another 5 minutes, or until the liquid has somewhat reduced. Drain. Add one teaspoon of oil and lemon juice.
2. Meanwhile, prepare the veggies: Heat the oil over medium heat in a large skillet. Add garlic and cook for 1 to 2 minutes, or until garlic is aromatic. Add roasted vegetables and cook, often turning, until vegetables are cooked through, for 2 to 4 minutes. Add and cook kale for 2 to 3 minutes, or until kale is barely wilted.
3. Add the pepper, coriander, and salt and mix well. Serve the veggies over the lentils with a dollop of tahini on top (or yogurt). If desired, garnish with parsley.

### PER SERVING

Calories: 453 kcal, Protein: 18.1 g, Carbohydrates: 49.7 g, Fat: 22.4 g, Cholesterol: 8.3 mg, Fiber: 5 g

## Tomato and Basil Quiche

**Prep time:10 minutes| Cook time:40 minutes| Serves 4**

- 2 cups of tomatoes, sliced
- 1 tablespoon of olive oil
- 2 tablespoons of flour
- 1 cup onion, sliced
- 2 teaspoons of dried basil
- 1/2 cup skim milk
- 3/4 cup egg substitute
- 1/2 teaspoon black pepper

- 1 cup Swiss cheese, shredded

1. Preheat the oven to 400 degrees Fahrenheit (200 degrees Celsius, or gas mark 6). In a large skillet, heat the olive oil over medium heat. Remove onion from skillet when it has softened. Cook for 1 minute on each side after sprinkling tomato slices with flour and basil.
2. Whisk together the egg substitute and milk in a small bowl. Season with salt and pepper. Half of the cheese should be spread in the bottom of a pie pan that has been coated with nonstick vegetable oil. Onions should be layered on top of the cheese, and tomatoes should be on top of that.
3. Over the vegetables, pour the egg mixture. The remaining cheese should be sprinkled on top. 10 minutes in the oven Bake for 15 to 20 minutes, or until the filling is puffy and golden brown, at 350°F (180°C, or gas mark 4). Warm the dish before serving.

### PER SERVING

Calories: 188 kcal, Protein: 18 g, Carbohydrates: 14 g, Fat: 7 g, Cholesterol:13 mg, Fiber: 2 g

## Vegetarian Bolognese

**Prep time:10 minutes| Cook time:4 hours 20 minutes| Serves 8**

- ½ cup of dry white wine
- 1 (28 ounces) can have diced San Marzano tomatoes,
- ½ cup of vegetable broth; low-sodium or water
- ½ cup of chopped celery
- 1 cup of chopped onion
- 3 tablespoons of olive oil; extra-virgin
- ½ cup of chopped carrot
- 1 teaspoon of Italian seasoning
- 2 tablespoons of minced garlic
- ¼ teaspoon of ground pepper
- ½ teaspoon of salt
- ¼ cup of heavy cream
- ¼ cup of chopped fresh basil.
- 2 (15 ounces) cans of cannellini beans; no-salt-added or rinsed small white beans,
- ½ cup of grated Parmesan cheese
- 1 pound of whole-wheat spaghetti

1. In a 5- to the 6-quart slow cooker, add wine, tomatoes, onion, celery, carrot, oil, garlic, broth (or water), salt, Italian seasoning, and pepper. Cook for 4 hours on high or 8 hours on low. At the end of the cooking time, add the cream and beans. Keep it warm.
2. Bring a big saucepan of water to a boil in the meanwhile. Drain pasta after cooking according to package instructions. Using 8 bowls, divide the spaghetti. Add the Parmesan, sauce, and basil to the top.

### PER SERVING

Calories: 434 kcal, Protein: 15.9 g, Carbohydrates: 64.3 g, Fat: 12.6 g, Cholesterol:12.1 mg, Fiber: 4 g

## Broccoli Wild Rice Casserole

**Prep time:10 minutes| Cook time:60 minutes| Serves 6**

- 1 1/2 cups wild rice
- 6 cups broccoli
- 2 cups reduced-sodium cream of mushroom soup
- 2 cups low fat cheddar cheese, shredded

1.  Preheat the oven to 325°F (170°C, or gas mark 3) before starting. Prepare wild rice as directed on the package.
2.  In the bottom of a 9 × 9-inch (23 x 23-cm) casserole pan, layer rice. Broccoli should be steamed for 5 minutes before being layered on top of rice.
3.  Toss the soup with the cheese and distribute it on top of the broccoli. Bake for 45 minutes, uncovered.

**PER SERVING**

Calories: 293 kcal, Protein: 20 g, Carbohydrates: 44 g, Fat: 5 g, Cholesterol:12 mg, Fiber: 5 g

## Grilled Eggplant and Tomato Pasta

**Prep time:5 minutes| Cook time:25 minutes| Serves 4**

- 2 teaspoons of chopped fresh oregano.
- 4 tablespoons of olive oil; extra-virgin, divided.
- 1 pound of chopped plum tomatoes,
- ½ teaspoon of ground pepper
- 1 grated clove of garlic,
- ½ teaspoon of salt
- ¼ teaspoon of crushed red pepper
- ½ cup of chopped fresh basil.
- 1½ pound of eggplant, 1/2-inch-thick slices
- ¼ cup of crumbled feta cheese or shaved Ricotta Salata
- 8 ounces of whole-wheat penne

1.  Bring a big saucepan of water to a boil. Preheat the grill to medium-high heat. In a large mixing bowl, combine 3 tablespoons of oil, crushed red pepper, tomatoes, garlic, pepper, oregano, and salt. Brush the remaining one tablespoon of oil over the eggplant. Grill for 4 minutes on each side, flipping once until cooked and browned in places.
2.  Allow 10 minutes for cooling. Chop them into bite-size pieces and add to the tomatoes with basils. In the meanwhile, prepare the pasta according to the package instructions. Drain. Toss the tomato mixture with the spaghetti and serve. Cheese should be sprinkled on top.

**PER SERVING**

Calories: 449 kcal, Protein: 13.5 g, Carbohydrates: 62.1 g, Fat: 19.2 g, Cholesterol: 8.3 mg, Fiber: 3 g

## Potato and Winter Vegetable Casserole

**Prep time:10 minutes| Cook time:30 minutes| Serves 6**

- 6 potatoes
- 2 tablespoons olive oil
- 1 cup onion, sliced
- 2 cups cabbage, chopped
- 2 cups cauliflower, chopped
- 1 teaspoon garlic, crushed
- 1 cup plain fat-free yogurt
- 2 cups canned white kidney beans
- 1/4 cup fresh dill, chopped
- 1/2 teaspoon paprika

1.  Preheat oven to 325°F (170°C, or gas mark 3). Boil or microwave the potatoes until nearly done. When cool enough, peel if desired. Heat the olive oil in a large skillet over medium-high heat. Sauté the onions until soft. Add the cabbage, cauliflower, garlic, and fry until the cabbage and cauliflower are tender.
2.  Add the yogurt to the vegetable mixture. Drain and rinse the white beans and add to the vegetable mixture. Mix thoroughly and set aside. Slice the potatoes into rounds and put half the slices on the bottom of a 9 x 13-inch (23 x 33-cm) baking dish sprayed with nonstick vegetable oil.
3.  Spread the vegetable mixture over the potatoes. Cover with the remaining potatoes. Sprinkle with dill and paprika. Bake for 20 minutes.

**PER SERVING**

Calories: 462 kcal, Protein: 17 g, Carbohydrates: 88 g, Fat: 6 g, Cholesterol: 1 mg, Fiber: 12 g

## Rainbow Grain Bowl and Cashew Tahini Sauce

**Prep time:20 minutes| Cook time:0 minutes| Serves 1**

- ¼ cup of packed parsley leaves
- ½ cup of water
- ¼ teaspoon of salt
- 1 tablespoon of cider vinegar or lemon juice
- ½ teaspoon of tamari or soy sauce; extra-virgin
- ¾ cup of unsalted cashews
- ½ cup of cooked lentils
- 1 tablespoon of olive oil; extra-virgin
- ¼ cup of grated raw beet
- ½ cup of cooked quinoa
- ¼ cup of chopped bell pepper
- ½ cup of shredded red cabbage
- ¼ cup of grated carrot
- For garnish,1 tablespoon of chopped toasted cashews.
- ¼ cup of sliced cucumber

1. Mix water, tamari (or soy sauce), cashews, lemon juice (or vinegar), oil, parsley, and salt in a blender.
2. In the middle of a shallow serving dish, combine lentils and quinoa. Cabbage, carrot, beet, pepper, and cucumber go on top. Two tablespoons of cashew sauce are spooned over the top (save the extra sauce for another use). If desired, garnish with cashews.

**PER SERVING**

Calories: 361 kcal, Protein: 16.6 g, Carbohydrates: 53.9 g, Fat: 10.1 g, Cholesterol: 1 mg, Fiber: 6 g

## Mexican Bean Bake

**Prep time:5 minutes| Cook time:20 minutes| Serves 6**

- 2 cups refried beans
- 4 cups cooked rice
- 2 cups canned black beans, drained
- 1 cup salsa
- 1 cup low-fat cheddar cheese, shredded

1. Preheat oven to 375°F (190°C, or gas mark 5). In a 9 x 9-inch (23 x 23-cm) baking dish, spread out the refried beans.
2. Layer cooked rice on top. Layer black beans on top of rice. Spread with salsa. Sprinkle with cheese. Bake for 15 to 20 minutes, or until heated through and cheese is melted.

**PER SERVING**

Calories: 334 kcal, Protein: 19 g, Carbohydrates: 57 g, Fat: 3 g, Cholesterol: 11 mg, Fiber: 11 g

## Chickpea and Potato Curry

**Prep time:5 minutes| Cook time:30 minutes| Serves 15**

- 3 tablespoons of canola oil or grapeseed oil
- 1 pound of peeled Yukon Gold potatoes, 1-inch pieces
- 3 minced cloves of garlic,
- 1 large, diced onion,
- ¾ teaspoon of salt
- 2 teaspoons of curry powder
- 1 (15 ounces) can of chickpeas, low-sodium, rinsed
- ¾ cup of water, divided.
- ½ teaspoon of garam masala
- 1 cup of frozen peas

1. In a large saucepan with a steamer basket, boil 1 inch of water. Add the potatoes, cover, and steam for 6 to 8 minutes, or until tender. Remove the potatoes and set them aside. Dry the pan.
2. In a medium-high-heat saucepan, heat the oil. Add onion and cook, often turning, until the onion is tender and transparent, for 3 to 5 minutes. Add and cook salt, curry powder, garlic, and cayenne, stirring continuously, for 1 minute, until fragrant. Cook for 2 minutes after adding the tomatoes and their juice. Fill a blender or food processor halfway with the mixture. Puree with 1/2 cup water until smooth.
3. Put the purée back in the saucepan. To rinse the sauce residue, pulse with the remaining 1/4 cup of water in the blender or food processor. Add the peas, chickpeas, saved potatoes, and gram masala to the pot. Cook for 5 minutes, often stirring, until heated.
4. Gram masala, a spice blend of coriander, cumin, black pepper, cinnamon, cardamom, and other spices, gives this Indian stew a warming, rich layer of flavor.

**PER SERVING**

Calories: 321 kcal, Protein: 8.9 g, Carbohydrates: 46.5 g, Fat: 11.5 g, Cholesterol: 3.8 mg, Fiber: 6 g

## Squash and Rice Bake

**Prep time:5 minutes| Cook time:40 minutes| Serves 4**

- 1/2 cup rice
- 2 tablespoons olive oil
- 1/4 teaspoon minced garlic
- 1/2 teaspoon dried thyme
- 2 ounces' low-fat Swiss cheese, shredded

1. Preheat oven to 350°F (180°C, or gas mark 4). Cook rice according to package directions. Heat oil in a large skillet. Sauté garlic for a few minutes. Add thyme and squash. Sauté for a few minutes more.
2. Stir the rice and cheese into the mixture. Turn into a 2-quart (1.9-L) baking dish that has been coated with nonstick vegetable oil spray. Bake for 25 minutes or until heated through.

**PER SERVING**

Calories: 128 kcal, Protein: 6 g, Carbohydrates: 10 g, Fat: 8 g, Cholesterol: 5 mg, Fiber: 1 g

## Zucchini Frittata

**Prep time:10 minutes| Cook time:20 minutes7| Serves 4**

- 2 cups shredded zucchini
- 2 tablespoons olive oil
- 1/2 cup mushrooms, sliced
- 1 cup egg substitute
- 1/3 cup Swiss cheese, shredded

1. Place the zucchini in a paper towel and squeeze out any excess moisture. Heat oil in a 10-inch (25-cm) skillet. Sauté the mushrooms briefly, then add the zucchini. Cook for 4 minutes, or until the squash is barely tender. Pour egg substitute over vegetables.
2. Stir once quickly to coat vegetables. Cook over low heat until eggs begin to set. Sprinkle with the cheese. Place under the broiler until cheese browns. Let set for 2 to 3 minutes. Cut into wedges and serve.

**PER SERVING**

Calories: 144 kcal, Protein: 12 g, Carbohydrates: 3 g, Fat: 10 g, Cholesterol: 4 mg, Fiber: 1 g

## Carrot Rice

**Prep time:10 minutes| Cook time:40 minutes| Serves 6**

- 2 cups of water
- 1 cup of basmati rice
- 1 tablespoon of margarine
- ¼ cup of roasted peanuts
- 1 sliced onion,
- ¾ cup of grated carrots
- 1 teaspoon of fresh minced ginger root
- salt to taste
- fresh chopped cilantro
- cayenne pepper; to taste.

1. In a medium saucepan, combine rice and water. Over high heat, bring to a boil. Reduce the heat to low, cover with a lid, and steam for 20 minutes, or until soft.
2. Grind the peanuts in a blender and put them aside. In a skillet, melt the margarine over medium heat. Add onion and cook, constantly stirring, for approximately 10 minutes, or until the onion is cooked and become golden brown. Add the ginger, carrots, and salt to taste. Reduce heat to low and cover for 5 minutes to steam. Add the peanuts and cayenne pepper and mix well. When the rice is done, pour it into the pan and gently mix it with the other ingredients. Serve with chopped cilantro as a garnish.

**PER SERVING**

Calories: 179 kcal, Protein: 4 g, Carbohydrates: 30.1 g, Fat: 4.8 g, Cholesterol: 3 mg, Fiber: 2 g

## Lentils and Pasta

**Prep time:10 minutes| Cook time:60 minutes| Serves 6**

- 1 cup lentils
- 1/2 cup celery, sliced
- 1 1/2 cups onion, coarsely chopped, divided
- 2 tablespoons olive oil
- 1/2 teaspoon cumin
- 1 tablespoon cilantro
- 6 ounces' fresh spinach
- 8 ounces pasta (small shapes like orzo are best)

1. Cook lentils in 6 cups (1.4 L) water with celery and 1 1/2 cups (80 g) of the onion until soft, about 40 minutes. Heat the olive oil and sauté the remaining onions, cumin, and cilantro until the onions are soft in a large skillet.
2. Add spinach and sauté until wilted, another 4 to 5 minutes. Drain lentils and stir into the onion-spinach mixture. Cook pasta according to package directions. Stir into mixture.

**PER SERVING**

Calories: 245 kcal, Protein: 10 g, Carbohydrates: 40 g, Fat: 5 g, Cholesterol: 0 mg, Fiber: 6 g

## Cheese Pie

**Prep time:10 minutes| Cook time:40 minutes| Serves 4**

- 4 ounces feta cheese
- 16 ounces low fat ricotta cheese
- 1 cup egg substitute
- 1/4 cup flour
- 3/4 cup skim milk
- 1/4 teaspoon black pepper

1. Preheat oven to 375°F (190°C, or gas mark 5). Spray an ovenproof skillet or glass baking dish with nonstick vegetable oil spray. Mix the cheeses, then stir in the egg substitute, flour, milk, and pepper.
2. Pour the batter into the prepared pan. Bake for 40 minutes, or until golden and set. Cut into wedges.

**PER SERVING**

Calories: 332 kcal, Protein: 27 g, Carbohydrates: 16 g, Fat: 17 g, Cholesterol: 62 mg, Fiber: 0 g

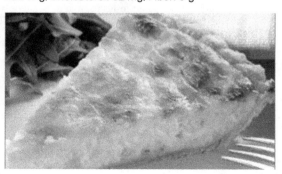

## Veggie and Hummus Sandwich

**Prep time: 10 minutes | Cook time: 0 minutes | Serves 1**

- ¼ medium sliced red bell pepper,
- 2 slices of whole-grain bread
- ¼ cup of sliced cucumber
- ¼ cup of shredded carrot
- 3 tablespoons of hummus
- ¼ mashed avocado,

1. Spread hummus on one piece of bread and avocado on the other. Greens, cucumber, bell pepper, and carrot are placed in the sandwich. Serve by slicing in half.

**PER SERVING**

Calories: 325 kcal, Protein: 12.8 g, Carbohydrates: 39.7 g, Fat: 14.3 g, Cholesterol: 0 mg, Fiber: 1 g

---

## Pasta Primavera

**Prep time: 10 minutes | Cook time: 30 minutes | Serves 6**

- 1 cup of sliced yellow squash or zucchini
- 1 cup of sliced mushrooms
- 2 cups of broccoli florets
- 2 cups of sliced green or red peppers
- 2 minced garlic cloves,
- 1/2 cup of chopped onion
- 1 cup of evaporated fat-free milk
- 1 teaspoon of butter
- 3/4 cup of Parmesan cheese; freshly grated.
- 1/3 cup of fresh finely chopped parsley.
- 12 ounces of whole-wheat pasta

1. Bring 1 inch of water to a boil in a big saucepan with a steamer basket. Add mushrooms, zucchini, broccoli, and peppers. Cover and steam for 10 minutes, or until tender-crisp. Remove the saucepan from the heat.
2. Heat the olive oil in a wide saucepan and sauté the garlic and onion over medium heat. Stir or shake the steamed veggies to evenly cover them in the garlic and onion mixture. Remove the pan from the heat but keep it warm.
3. Heat the milk, butter, and Parmesan cheese in a separate wide pot. Stir constantly over low heat until the sauce has thickened and cooked thoroughly. Stir constantly to avoid scalding. Remove the pan from the heat but keep it warm.
4. Fill a big saucepan 3/4 full of water and bring to a boil in the meanwhile. Cook pasta for 10 to 12 minutes, or according to package instructions, until the pasta is al dente (tender). Drain all of the water from the pasta.
5. Distribute the spaghetti equally among the plates. Pour the sauce over the after topping with vegetables. Serve immediately with fresh parsley as a garnish.

**PER SERVING**

Calories: 347 kcal, Protein: 17 g, Carbohydrates: 54 g, Fat: 7 g, Cholesterol: 12 mg, Fiber: 4 g

---

## Loaded Veggie-Stuffed Peppers

**Prep time: 15 minutes | Cook time: 1 hour | Makes 6 Peppers**

- ½ cup brown rice, rinsed
- 1 cup water
- 1 (19-ounce) can low-sodium black beans, drained and rinsed
- 1 (12-ounce) can low-sodium corn, drained
- 1 cup fresh lime salsa
- 6 orange bell peppers, halved top to bottom and seeded
- olive oil

1. In a medium saucepan over high heat, combine the rice and water and bring to a boil. Cover, reduce the heat to low, and simmer until the liquid is absorbed, about 30 minutes. Remove from the heat, fluff with a fork, and let cool.
2. Preheat the oven to 375°F. Line a baking sheet with parchment paper.
3. In a medium bowl, combine the rice, black beans, corn, and Fresh Lime Salsa.
4. Lightly brush the outside of the bell pepper halves with oil.
5. Evenly distribute the bean mixture among the bell pepper halves. Place the peppers on the prepared baking sheet and cover them with aluminum foil.
6. Bake the stuffed peppers for 20 minutes, remove the foil, and bake for another 10 minutes until fragrant. Enjoy immediately.

**PER SERVING (1 PEPPER)**

Calories: 279; Total fat: 3g; Saturated fat: 0g; Trans fat: 0g; Protein: 11g; Total carbohydrate: 56g; Fiber: 10g; Sodium: 122mg; Potassium: 1,201mg.

# Chapter 10
# Soups and Stews

## Healthy Minestrone

**Prep time: 12 minutes | Cook time: 18 minutes | Serves 4**

- 1 tablespoon olive oil
- 1 onion, chopped
- 2 cloves garlic, minced
- 1 red bell pepper, seeded and chopped
- 1 cup chopped red cabbage
- 1 (15-ounce can) low-sodium cannellini beans, rinsed and drained
- 1 (14-ounce) can no-salt-added diced tomatoes, undrained
- 3 cups low-sodium vegetable broth
- 1 teaspoon dried basil leaves
- ½ teaspoon dried oregano leaves
- ½ teaspoon dried thyme leaves
- Pinch salt
- ⅛ teaspoon black pepper
- ½ cup whole-wheat elbow macaroni
- 2 cups baby spinach leaves
- ¼ cup shredded Parmesan

1. In a large saucepan, heat the olive oil over medium heat.
2. Add the onion and garlic, and cook and stir for 3 minutes. Add the red bell pepper and cabbage, and cook and stir for 2 minutes longer.
3. Add the beans, tomatoes, broth, basil, oregano, thyme, salt, and pepper. Simmer for 3 minutes.
4. Stir in the macaroni and simmer for 7 to 9 minutes more, or until the pasta is cooked al dente.
5. 5.Stir in the spinach leaves until they wilt, about 1 minute. Serve, topped with the Parmesan cheese.

**PER SERVING**

Calories 290; Fat 6g (with 18% calories from fat); Saturated fat 1g; Monounsaturated fat 3g; Carbs 45g; Sodium 188mg; Dietary fiber 11g; Protein 16g; Cholesterol 5mg; Vitamin A 40% DV; Vitamin C 125% DV; Sugar 7g

## Quinoa Vegetable Soup

**Prep time: 10 minutes | Cook time: 20 minutes | Serves 4**

- 2 teaspoons olive oil
- 1 leek, white and light-green parts, chopped and rinsed
- 3 cloves garlic, minced
- 2 carrots, sliced ½-inch thick
- 3 cups low-sodium vegetable broth
- 2 tomatoes, chopped
- ¾ cup quinoa, rinsed and drained
- 1 sprig fresh rosemary
- 1 sprig fresh thyme
- Pinch salt
- ⅛ teaspoon cayenne pepper
- 1 cup baby spinach leaves

1. In a large saucepan, heat the olive oil over medium heat.
2. Add the leek and garlic, and cook and stir for 2

minutes.
3. Add the carrot, broth, tomatoes, quinoa, rosemary, thyme, salt, and cayenne pepper, and bring to a simmer.
4. Reduce the heat to low, partially cover the pan, and simmer for 17 to 19 minutes, or until the vegetables and quinoa are tender. Stir in the spinach.
5. Remove the rosemary and thyme sprigs, and serve.

**PER SERVING**

Calories 191; Fat 6g (with 28% calories from fat); Saturated fat 1g; Monounsaturated fat 2g; Carbs 32g; Sodium 142mg; Dietary fiber 5g; Protein 6g; Cholesterol 0mg; Vitamin A 134% DV; Vitamin C 25% DV; Sugar 6g

## German Potato Soup

**Prep time: 10 minutes | Cook time: 20 minutes | Serves 4**

- 2 teaspoons olive oil
- 2 onions, chopped
- 4 cloves garlic, minced
- 2 large Yukon Gold potatoes, rinsed and chopped
- 2 cups low-sodium vegetable broth
- 1 tablespoon low-sodium yellow mustard
- 1 teaspoon tamari sauce
- 1 tablespoon chopped fresh rosemary leaves
- ½ teaspoon dried sage leaves
- ¼ cup plain low-fat Greek yogurt
- ¼ cup grated extra sharp cheddar cheese
- ⅓ cup chopped fresh flat-leaf parsley
- ¼ cup vegan bacon bits (optional)

1. In a large saucepan, heat the olive oil over medium heat.
2. Add the onions and garlic, and cook and stir for 3 minutes.
3. Add the potatoes, vegetable broth, mustard, tamari, rosemary, and sage, and bring to a simmer. Simmer for 14 to 17 minutes or until the potatoes are tender.
4. At this point, some of the soup needs to be puréed, and there are many methods you can choose from. You can do this with an immersion blender, leaving some of the potato chunks whole if you'd like. You can use a potato masher right in the pot. Or put half of the soup into a blender, cover the blender with the lid and a towel, and blend until smooth. Then pour the blended mixture back into the soup. After you have puréed the soup, stir in the yogurt and cheddar cheese.
5. Simmer the soup for 1 minute, then ladle into bowls. Garnish with the parsley and vegan bacon bits, if using.

**PER SERVING**

Calories 223; Fat 5g (with 20% calories from fat); Saturated fat 2g; Monounsaturated fat 2g; Carbs 37g; Sodium 208mg; Dietary fiber 6g; Protein 8g; Cholesterol 8mg; Vitamin A 7% DV; Vitamin C 31% DV; Sugar 5g

## Pumpkin Soup with Crunchy Seeds

**Prep time:15 minutes | Cook time: 15 minutes| Serves 4**

- 2 teaspoons olive oil, divided
- 1 onion, chopped
- 1 tablespoon fresh peeled grated ginger root
- 1 (15-ounce) can pumpkin
- 2 cups low-sodium chicken stock
- 1 cup unsweetened apple juice
- ⅓ cup natural unsweetened applesauce
- Pinch salt
- 3 tablespoons raw shelled pumpkin seeds
- 2 teaspoons brown sugar
- ⅛ teaspoon cayenne pepper

1. Heat 1 teaspoon of the olive oil in a large saucepan over medium heat.
2. Add the onion and ginger root, and cook and stir for 2 minutes.
3. Turn up the heat to medium-high and add the pumpkin, chicken stock, apple juice, applesauce, and salt. Stir and bring to a boil.
4. Reduce the heat to low and simmer for 10 to 12 minutes, stirring occasionally.
5. Meanwhile, in a small saucepan, combine the remaining 1 teaspoon olive oil, the pumpkin seeds, brown sugar, and cayenne pepper. Heat over medium heat, stirring frequently, until the seeds are caramelized. Transfer them to a small bowl.
6. Serve the soup topped with the pumpkin seeds.

**PER SERVING**

Calories 149; Fat 6g (with 36% calories from fat); Saturated fat 1g; Monounsaturated fat 3g; Carbs 24g; Sodium 84mg; Dietary fiber 4g; Protein 4g; Cholesterol 0mg; Vitamin A 413% DV; Vitamin C 40% DV; Sugar 14g

## Butternut Squash and Lentil Soup

**Prep time:10 minutes | Cook time: 20 minutes| Serves 4**

- 1 tablespoon olive oil
- 1 onion, chopped
- 1 tablespoon peeled grated fresh ginger root
- 1 (12-ounce) package peeled and diced butternut squash
- 1 cup red lentils, rinsed and sorted
- 5 cups low-sodium vegetable broth
- 1 cup unsweetened apple juice
- Pinch salt
- ⅛ teaspoon black pepper
- ¼ teaspoon curry powder
- 1 sprig fresh thyme
- 3 tablespoons crumbled blue cheese

1. In a large saucepan, heat the olive oil over medium heat. Add the onion, and cook and stir for 3 minutes. Add the ginger, squash, and lentils, and cook and stir for 1 minute.
2. Turn up the heat to medium-high, and add the broth, apple juice, salt, pepper, curry powder, and

thyme. Bring the mixture to a boil.
3. Reduce the heat to low and partially cover the pan. Simmer for 15 to 18 minutes or until the squash and lentils are tender. Remove the thyme sprig; the leaves will have fallen off.
4. Purée the soup, either in a food processor, with an immersion blender, or with a potato masher. Heat again, then ladle into bowls, sprinkle with the blue cheese, and serve warm.

**PER SERVING**

Calories 317; Fat 7g (with 20% calories from fat); Saturated fat 2g; Monounsaturated fat 3g; Carbs 52g; Sodium 280mg; Dietary fiber 9g; Protein 15g; Cholesterol 5mg; Vitamin A 180% DV; Vitamin C 74% DV; Sugar 12g

## Spicy Lentil Chili

**Prep time:10 minutes | Cook time: 20 minutes| Serves 4**

- 1 tablespoon olive oil
- 1 onion, chopped
- 5 cloves garlic, minced
- 1 jalapeño pepper, seeded and minced
- 1 cup red lentils, sorted and rinsed
- 1 tablespoon chili powder
- 1 teaspoon smoked paprika
- ⅛ teaspoon red pepper flakes
- 1 (14-ounce) can no-salt-added diced tomatoes, undrained
- 3 tablespoons no-salt-added tomato paste
- 1 (16-ounce) can low-sodium kidney beans, rinsed and drained
- ⅓ cup chopped fresh cilantro leaves

1. In a large saucepan, heat the olive oil over medium heat.
2. Add the onion, garlic, and jalapeño pepper, and cook and stir for 2 minutes.
3. Add the lentils, chili powder, paprika, red pepper flakes, tomatoes, tomato paste, and kidney beans, and bring to a boil.
4. Lower the heat, partially cover the pan, and simmer for 15 to 18 minutes, or until the chili powder has blended in and the lentils are tender. Top with the fresh cilantro and serve.

**PER SERVING**

Calories 364; Fat 5g (with 12% calories from fat); Saturated fat 1g; Monounsaturated fat 2g; Carbs 59g; Sodium 130mg; Dietary fiber 26g; Protein 22g; Cholesterol 0mg; Vitamin A 31% DV; Vitamin C 21% DV; Sugar 8g

## Three Bean Soup

**Prep time:10 minutes | Cook time: 20 minutes | Serves 4**

- 1 tablespoon olive oil
- 1 leek, white and light-green parts, chopped and rinsed
- 1 carrot, thinly sliced
- 1 (16-ounce) can low-sodium black beans, rinsed and drained
- 2 cups green beans, cut into 1-inch pieces
- 1 cup frozen shelled edamame
- 3 cups low-sodium vegetable broth
- 1 (14-ounce) can no-salt-added diced tomatoes
- 1 teaspoon dried basil leaves
- 1 teaspoon dried oregano leaves
- Pinch salt
- ⅛ teaspoon black pepper

1. In a large saucepan or stockpot, heat the olive oil over medium heat.
2. Add the leek, and cook and stir for 4 minutes. Add the carrot, and cook and stir for 1 minute.
3. Add the black beans, green beans, edamame, vegetable broth, tomatoes, basil, oregano, salt, and pepper, stir to combine, and bring to a boil.
4. Reduce the heat to low, partially cover the pan, and simmer for 15 minutes or until the vegetables are tender. Serve.

**PER SERVING**

Calories 245; Fat 6g (with 22% calories from fat); Saturated fat 1g; Monounsaturated fat 2g; Carbs 35g; Sodium 260mg; Dietary fiber 13g; Protein 16g; Cholesterol 0mg; Vitamin A 78% DV; Vitamin C 34% DV; Sugar 8g

## Curried Cauliflower Stew

**Prep time:15 minutes | Cook time: 15 minutes | Serves 4**

- 1 tablespoon olive oil
- 2 shallots, minced
- 1 tablespoon curry powder
- 2 cloves garlic, minced
- 2 carrots, sliced
- 1 head cauliflower, cut into florets and chopped
- ⅛ teaspoon white pepper
- 3 cups low-sodium vegetable broth
- 1 (14-ounce) can no-salt-added diced tomatoes, undrained
- 1 (15-ounce) can no-salt-added cannellini beans, rinsed and drained
- ½ cup chopped fresh flat-leaf parsley

1. Heat the olive oil in a large saucepan over medium heat. Add the shallots, curry powder, and garlic, and cook and stir for 1 minute.
2. Add the carrots, cauliflower florets, white pepper, vegetable broth, tomatoes, and beans, and bring to a boil over medium heat.
3. Reduce the heat, partially cover the pot, and simmer for 13 to 14 minutes or until the cauliflower

is tender.
4. Using a potato masher, mash some of the soup in the pot so it thickens. Top with the fresh parsley and serve.

**PER SERVING**

Calories 247; Fat 5g (with 18% calories from fat); Saturated fat 1g; Monounsaturated fat 3g; Carbs 42g; Sodium 182mg; Dietary fiber 13g; Protein 13g; Cholesterol 0mg; Vitamin A 118% DV; Vitamin C 144% DV; Sugar 8g

## Gazpacho

**Prep time:20 minutes | Serves 4**

- 4 large beefsteak tomatoes, chopped
- 1 cup yellow or red cherry tomatoes, chopped
- 1 cup grape tomatoes, chopped
- 1 cucumber, peeled, seeded, and chopped
- 3 scallions, sliced
- 1 clove garlic, minced
- 1 cup low-sodium tomato juice
- 1 tablespoon fresh lemon juice
- 1 tablespoon olive oil
- Pinch salt
- ⅛ teaspoon white pepper
- dash tabasco sauce
- 2 tablespoons chopped fresh dill

1. In a large bowl, combine the beefsteak tomatoes, cherry tomatoes, grape tomatoes, cucumber, scallions, garlic, tomato juice, lemon juice, olive oil, salt, white pepper, Tabasco, and fresh dill.
2. Use an immersion blender to blend about half of the soup. You can also mash some of the ingredients with a potato masher. Or put about ⅓ of the soup mixture into a blender or food processor. Blend or process until smooth, then return the blended mixture to the rest of the soup.
3. Serve immediately, or cover and chill for a few hours.

**PER SERVING**

Calories 115; Fat 4g (with 31% calories from fat); Saturated fat 1g; Monounsaturated fat 2g; Carbs 19g; Sodium 225mg; Dietary fiber 5g; Protein 4g; Cholesterol 0mg; Vitamin A 65% DV; Vitamin C 137% DV; Sugar 12g

## Carrot Peach Soup

**Prep time:15 minutes | Cook time: 15 minutes| Serves 4**

- 2 large carrots, peeled and chopped
- 2 peaches, peeled and chopped (see Ingredient Tip)
- 2 cups water
- ½ cup orange juice
- 2 tablespoons honey
- 1 sprig fresh thyme leaves
- Pinch salt
- ⅓ cup plain low-fat Greek yogurt

1.  In a large saucepan, combine the carrots, peaches, water, orange juice, honey, thyme, and salt, and bring to a simmer over medium heat.
2.  Simmer the mixture for 7 to 9 minutes or until the carrots are tender.
3.  Add the yogurt to the soup and remove the thyme sprig. Purée the soup, either with an immersion blender directly in the pot, or pour the soup in two batches into a blender or food processor, and holding a towel over the lid, carefully blend until smooth. Serve immediately or cover and chill for 2 hours.

**PER SERVING**

Calories 102; Fat 0g (with 0% calories from fat); Saturated fat 0g; Monounsaturated fat 0g; Carbs 23g; Sodium 77mg; Dietary fiber 2g; Protein 3g; Cholesterol 0mg; Vitamin A 130% DV; Vitamin C 41% DV; Sugar 21g

## Tuscan Fish Stew

**Prep time:10 minutes | Cook time: 20 minutes| Serves 4**

- 1 tablespoon olive oil
- 1 onion, chopped
- 2 cloves garlic, minced
- 3 large tomatoes, chopped
- 1 bulb fennel, peeled, chopped, and rinsed
- 1 (14-ounce) can artichoke hearts, drained
- 1 bay leaf
- ⅛ teaspoon red pepper flakes
- 2 cups low-sodium vegetable broth
- ¾ pound halibut fillets, cubed
- ¼ pound sea scallops
- 1 slice low-sodium whole-wheat bread, crumbled
- 2 tablespoons chopped fresh basil
- 2 teaspoons chopped fresh oregano
- 2 tablespoons chopped fresh flat-leaf parsley

1.  In a stockpot or large saucepan, heat the olive oil over medium heat.
2.  Add the onion and garlic, and cook while stirring for 3 minutes.
3.  Add the tomatoes, fennel, artichoke hearts, bay leaf, red pepper flakes, and vegetable broth, and bring to a simmer. Simmer for 5 minutes.
4.  Add the halibut fillets, and simmer for 4 minutes. Then add the scallops, and simmer for 3 minutes, or until the fillets flake when tested with a fork

and the scallops are opaque.
5.  Stir in the bread crumbs, then cover the pan and remove from the heat. Let stand 3 minutes.
6.  Remove and discard the bay leaf. Top the soup with the fresh basil, oregano, and parsley, and serve.

**PER SERVING**

Calories 210; Fat 6g (with 26% calories from fat); Saturated fat 1g; Monounsaturated fat 2g; Carbs 28g; Sodium 247mg; Dietary fiber 10g; Protein 29g; Cholesterol 9mg; Vitamin A 24% DV; Vitamin C 43% DV; Sugar 6g

## Cioppino

**Prep time:10 minutes | Cook time: 20 minutes| Serves 4**

- 2 teaspoons olive oil
- 1 leek, white and light-green parts, chopped and rinsed
- 3 cloves garlic, minced
- 3 stalks celery, sliced ½ inch thick
- 1 bay leaf
- ½ teaspoon dried oregano leaves
- ⅛ teaspoon cayenne pepper
- 3 cups low-sodium vegetable broth
- ¼ cup white wine (optional)
- 1 (14-ounce) can no-salt-added diced tomatoes, undrained
- ½ pound red snapper fillets, cubed
- ¼ pound medium shrimp, peeled and deveined
- ¼ cup bay scallops
- ¼ pound mussels, cleaned
- 2 tablespoons fresh lemon juice
- ½ cup chopped fresh flat-leaf parsley

1.  Heat the olive oil in a soup pot over medium heat.
2.  Add the leek and garlic, and cook and stir for 3 minutes. Add the celery and cook for 1 minute longer.
3.  Add the bay leaf, oregano, cayenne pepper, vegetable broth, wine (if using), and tomatoes. Bring to a simmer, and simmer for 5 minutes.
4.  Add the red snapper, and simmer for 3 minutes. Add the shrimp, and simmer for 2 minutes longer. Then add the scallops and mussels. Simmer for 2 minutes longer, or until the mussels open and the shrimp curl and turn pink.
5.  Remove and discard the bay leaf. Add the lemon juice, and sprinkle with the parsley. Serve hot.

**PER SERVING**

Calories 220; Fat 5g (with 20% calories from fat); Saturated fat 1g; Monounsaturated fat 3g; Carbs 13g; Sodium 278mg; Dietary fiber 2g; Protein 30g; Cholesterol 95mg; Vitamin A 24% DV; Vitamin C 52% DV; Sugar 5g

## Salmon Veggie Chowder

**Prep time:15 minutes | Cook time: 15 minutes| Serves 4**

- 2 teaspoons olive oil
- 1 onion, chopped
- 2 cloves garlic, minced
- 1 carrot, sliced
- 1 sweet potato, peeled and chopped
- 3 cups low-sodium fish broth or vegetable broth
- 1 teaspoon dried marjoram leaves
- Pinch salt
- ⅛ teaspoon black pepper
- 2 (6-ounce) skinless salmon fillets
- 1 cup frozen corn, thawed
- 1 cup low-fat milk
- 2 tablespoons corn starch

1. In a large saucepan, heat the olive oil over medium heat. Add the onion and garlic, and cook and stir for 3 minutes.
2. Add the carrot, sweet potato, broth, marjoram, salt, and pepper, and bring to a simmer.
3. Simmer for 7 to 8 minutes, or until the vegetables are soft.
4. Add the salmon fillets to the soup, and simmer for 3 to 4 minutes, or until the salmon flakes when tested with a fork.
5. Remove the salmon from the pot and flake into large pieces. Return to the pot along with the corn and simmer for 1 minute.
6. In a small bowl combine the milk and cornstarch. Whisk until blended. Add to the soup and simmer for 1 minute or until the soup is thickened. Serve.

**PER SERVING**

Calories 333; Fat 13g (with 35% calories from fat); Saturated fat 3g; Monounsaturated fat 2g; Carbs 29g; Sodium 213mg; Dietary fiber 4g; Protein 26g; Cholesterol 52mg; Vitamin A 346% DV; Vitamin C 14% DV; Sugar 10g

## Chicken Vegetable Stew

**Prep time:10 minutes | Cook time: 20 minutes| Serves 4**

- 2 teaspoons olive oil
- 3 (4-ounce) boneless, skinless chicken thighs, cubed
- Pinch salt
- ⅛ teaspoon black pepper
- 1 onion, chopped
- 2 cloves garlic, minced
- 2 carrots, chopped
- 1 sweet potato, rinsed and chopped
- 2 cups low-sodium chicken stock
- 1 cup water
- 1 cup frozen corn
- 1 cup frozen shelled edamame
- 1 teaspoon dried Italian seasoning
- 1 cup stemless torn kale leaves or baby spinach leaves
- 1 tablespoon fresh lemon juice

1. Heat the olive oil in a large saucepan over medium heat.

2. Sprinkle the chicken with salt and pepper, and add to the saucepan. Cook the chicken, stirring frequently, until it is browned, about 4 to 5 minutes.
3. Remove the chicken from the pan and set aside.
4. Add the onion and garlic to the pan, and cook for 2 minutes, stirring frequently. Add the carrots, sweet potato, chicken stock, water, corn, edamame, and Italian seasoning, and bring to a simmer.
5. Return the chicken to the pan; simmer for 10 to 13 minutes, or until the vegetables are tender and the chicken is cooked to 165°F when tested with a meat thermometer.
6. Add the kale and cook for 1 minute longer. Stir in the lemon juice, and serve.

**PER SERVING**

Calories 256; Fat 10g (with 35% calories from fat); Saturated fat 2g; Monounsaturated fat 4g; Carbs 15g; Sodium mg; Dietary fiber 5g; Protein 28g; Cholesterol 72mg; Vitamin A 354% DV; Vitamin C 28% DV; Sugar 3g

## Thai Chicken Soup

**Prep time:10 minutes | Cook time: 20 minutes|Serves 4**

- 2 teaspoons olive oil
- 2 (6-ounce) boneless, skinless chicken breasts
- Pinch salt
- ⅛ teaspoon cayenne pepper
- 1 jalapeño chile, seeded and minced
- 1 red bell pepper, seeded and chopped
- 2 cups low-sodium chicken stock
- 1 cup water
- 2 tablespoons fresh lime juice
- 1 teaspoon Thai chili paste
- ⅛ teaspoon ground ginger

1. In a large saucepan, heat the olive oil over medium heat.
2. Sprinkle the chicken with the salt and cayenne pepper, and add it to the saucepan. Cook, turning once, until the chicken is browned, about 3 to 4 minutes per side. Transfer the chicken to a plate and set aside.
3. Add the lemongrass, garlic, jalapeño, and bell pepper to the saucepan, and cook for 3 minutes, stirring frequently.
4. Add the chicken stock and water to the saucepan, and stir and bring to a simmer. Return the chicken to the saucepan. Simmer for 10 to 12 minutes, or until the chicken is cooked to 165°F when tested with a meat thermometer.
5. Remove the chicken to a clean plate and shred, using two forks. Return the chicken to the soup.
6. Add the lime juice, chili paste, and ginger, and simmer for 2 minutes longer. Serve hot.

**PER SERVING**

Calories 134; Fat 5g (with 34% calories from fat); Saturated fat 1g; Monounsaturated fat 2g; Carbs 4g; Sodium 237mg; Dietary fiber 1g; Protein 20g; Cholesterol 49mg; Vitamin A % DV; Vitamin C % DV; Sugar 2g

## Healthy Bean Soup

**Prep time: 10 minutes | Cook time: 6 hours | Serves 6**

- 1 lb dried great northern beans, soak overnight & drained
- 2 cups water
- 4 cups vegetable broth
- ½ tsp dried sage
- 1 tbsp garlic, minced
- 1 yellow onion, diced
- 2 celery stalks, diced
- 2 large carrots, diced
- Pepper
- Salt

1. Add beans and remaining ingredients into the slow cooker and stir well.
2. Cover and cook on high for 6 hours.
3. Stir well and serve.

**PER SERVING**

Calories 281; Fat 1 g ;Carbohydrates 52.5 g ;Sugar 4.2 g;Protein 17.3 g; Cholesterol 0 mg

## Thick & Creamy Potato Soup

**Prep time: 10 minutes | Cook time: 6 hours | Serves 6**

- 6 cups sweet potatoes, diced
- ¼ tsp cinnamon
- ¼ tsp nutmeg
- ½ cup peanut butter, creamy
- 4 cups vegetable broth
- 1 tbsp ginger garlic paste
- 1 onion, diced
- Pepper
- Salt

1. Add sweet potatoes and remaining ingredients into the slow cooker and stir well.
2. Cover and cook on low for 6 hours.
3. Puree the soup using a blender until smooth.
4. Stir well and serve.

**PER SERVING**

Calories 201 ;Fat 1.3 g ;Carbohydrates 45 g ;Sugar 2.1 g ;Protein 3.2 g ;Cholesterol 0 mg

## Nutritious Broccoli Soup

**Prep time: 10 minutes | Cook time: 15 minutes | Serves 4**

- 3 cups broccoli florets
- 2 tbsp fresh lemon juice
- 3 ½ cups vegetable broth
- 2 potatoes, chopped
- 2 tbsp olive oil
- 1 ½ tbsp garlic, minced
- Pepper
- Salt

1. Heat oil into the pot over medium heat.
2. Add garlic, potatoes, and broccoli florets and sauté for 5 minutes.
3. Add broth, pepper, and salt and stir well. Bring to boil.
4. Turn heat to low and simmer for 10 minutes. Remove pot from heat.
5. Puree the soup using a blender until smooth.
6. Serve and enjoy.

**PER SERVING**

Calories 172 ;Fat 7.5 g ;Carbohydrates 25 g ;Sugar 3.4 g ;Protein 4.3 g ;Cholesterol 0 mg

## Easy Pea Soup

**Prep time: 10 minutes | Cook time: 20 minutes | Serves 6**

- 2 cups split peas
- 8 cups vegetable broth
- 1 tsp dried oregano
- 1 tbsp garlic, chopped
- 2 carrots, chopped
- 2 celery stalks, chopped
- 1 tbsp sesame oil
- 1 onion, chopped
- Pepper
- Salt

1. Add oil into the instant pot and set the pot on sauté mode.
2. Add carrots, celery, onion, and sauté for 5 minutes. Season with pepper and salt. Turn off sauté mode.
3. Add remaining ingredients and stir well.
4. Cover and cook on high for 15 minutes.
5. Once cooking is done, then allow releasing pressure naturally. Remove lid.
6. Puree the soup using a blender until smooth.
7. Serve and enjoy.

**PER SERVING**

Calories 314 ;Fat 5 g ;Carbohydrates 45.3 g ;Sugar 8.1 g ;Protein 23.1 g ;Cholesterol 0 mg

## Gluten-Free Asparagus Soup

**Prep time: 10 minutes | Cook time: 20 minutes | Serves 4**

- 1 ½ lbs asparagus, trimmed & chopped
- 4 cups vegetable broth
- 14 oz can white beans, drained & rinsed
- 1 tbsp sesame oil
- 1 tsp garlic, chopped
- 1 onion, chopped
- Pepper
- Salt

1. Heat oil into the pot over medium heat.
2. Add onion and sauté for 4 minutes. Add garlic and sauté for a minute.
3. Add remaining ingredients and stir well. Bring to boil.
4. Turn heat to low and simmer for 10 minutes. Remove pot from heat.
5. Puree the soup using a blender until smooth.
6. Stir well and serve.

**PER SERVING**

Calories 172 ;Fat 4.6 g ;Carbohydrates 25 g ;Sugar 5.9 g ;Protein 10.2 g ;Cholesterol 0 mg

## Flavors Corn Soup

**Prep time: 10 minutes | Cook time: 8 hours | Serves 8**

- 20 oz can corn, drained
- 3 cups vegetable broth
- 1/2 tsp coriander powder
- ½ tsp thyme
- 1 tsp cumin powder
- 1 ½ jalapeno pepper, seeded & chopped
- 2 large potatoes, cut into chunks
- Pepper
- Salt

1. Add corn and remaining ingredients into the slow cooker and stir everything well.
2. Cover and cook on low for 8 hours.
3. Stir well and serve.

**PER SERVING**

Calories 125 ;Fat 0.9 g ;Carbohydrates 28.5 g ;Sugar 3.6 g ;Protein 3.7 g ;Cholesterol 0 mg

## Healthy Mushroom Soup

**Prep time: 10 minutes | Cook time: 5 minutes | Serves 1**

- ¼ cup mushrooms, chopped
- ½ cup unsweetened almond milk
- ¾ cup vegetable broth
- 2 tbsp olive oil
- 3 tbsp rice flour
- Pepper
- Salt

1. Heat oil into the saucepan over medium heat.
2. Add mushrooms and sauté until softened.
3. Add flour and cook for a minute. Add broth and milk and stir well.
4. Turn heat to low and simmer until thickened. Season with pepper and salt.
5. Stir well and serve.

**PER SERVING**

Calories 377 ;Fat 30.3 g ;Carbohydrates 26.1 g ;Sugar 0.9 g ;Protein 3.1 g ;Cholesterol 0 mg

## Potato Squash Soup

**Prep time: 10 minutes | Cook time: 22 minutes | Serves 4**

- 2 large summer squash, cut into half
- 2 tbsp fresh lemon juice
- ½ cup unsweetened coconut milk
- 4 cups vegetable broth
- 1 tbsp olive oil
- 1 tsp garlic, minced
- 1 potato, peeled & diced
- 1 yellow onion, diced
- Pepper
- Salt

1. Heat oil into the pot over medium heat.
2. Add all veggies and sauté for 5 minutes.
3. Add broth and stir well, and bring to boil.
4. Turn heat to low and simmer vegetables for 15-20 minutes. Remove from heat.
5. Puree the soup using a blender until smooth.
6. Stir in lemon juice and coconut milk. Season with pepper and salt.
7. Serve and enjoy.

**PER SERVING**

Calories 200 ;Fat 12.3 g ;Carbohydrates 17.1 g ;Sugar 5.8 g ;Protein 7.5 g ;Cholesterol 0 mg

## Silky Zucchini Soup

**Prep time: 10 minutes | Cook time: 30 minutes | Serves 4**

- 6 cups zucchini, chopped
- 1½ cups vegetable broth
- 1 tbsp olive oil
- 1 tbsp garlic, minced
- 1 medium onion, chopped
- ¼ tsp chili powder
- Pepper
- Salt

1. Heat oil into the pot over medium heat.
2. Add onion and sauté for 5 minutes.
3. Add garlic and sauté for a minute.
4. Add zucchini, chili powder, pepper, and salt and sauté for 10 minutes.
5. Add broth and stir well, reduce heat and simmer for 15 minutes.
6. Puree the soup using a blender until smooth.
7. Serve and enjoy.

**PER SERVING**

Calories 74 ;Fat 3.9 g ;Carbohydrates 9.4 g ;Sugar 4.4 g ;Protein 2.7 g ;Cholesterol 0 mg

## Flavors Vegetable Stew

**Prep time: 10 minutes | Cook time: 8 hours | Serves 6**

- 1 cup frozen peas
- 1 cup frozen corn
- 2 lbs potatoes, peeled & cubed
- 4 large carrots, peeled & diced
- 1 medium onion, chopped
- ½ cup unsweetened coconut milk
- ½ tsp dried oregano
- 1 tsp garlic powder
- 4 cups vegetable broth
- Pepper
- Salt

1. Add all ingredients except coconut milk into the slow cooker and stir well.
2. Cover and cook on low for 8 hours.
3. Stir in coconut milk and serve.

**PER SERVING**

Calories 226 ;Fat 5.4 g ;Carbohydrates 40.9 g ;Sugar 8.2 g ;Protein 6.2 g ;Cholesterol 0 mg

## Chickpea Sweet Potato Stew

**Prep time: 10 minutes | Cook time: 4hours 5 minutes | Serves 4**

- 2 medium sweet potatoes, chopped
- 14 oz can chickpeas, drained & rinsed
- 1/8 tsp cayenne
- ½ tsp turmeric
- ½ tsp cinnamon
- 1 tsp smoked paprika
- 1½ tsp garam masala
- 1 tsp ground coriander
- 1 cup vegetable broth
- 2 cups canned tomatoes, crushed
- 1 tbsp garlic, chopped
- 1 tbsp olive oil
- 1 onion, chopped
- Pepper
- Salt

1. Heat oil in a pan over medium-high heat.
2. Add onion and sauté for 3 minutes.
3. Add garlic and sauté for a minute.
4. Transfer sautéed onion and remaining ingredients into the slow cooker and stirred well.
5. Cover and cook on high for 4 hours.
6. Stir well and serve.

**PER SERVING**

Calories 283 ;Fat 5.1 g ;Carbohydrates 53.8 g ;Sugar 5.8 g ;Protein 7.9 g ;Cholesterol 0 mg

## Lentil Veggie Stew

**Prep time: 10 minutes | Cook time: 4 hours | Serves 8**

- 1 cup green lentils, rinsed
- ¼ cup olive oil
- ¼ tsp chili powder
- ½ tsp dried thyme
- ½ tsp dried oregano
- ½ cup wheat berries
- 4 cups vegetable broth
- 1 tsp garlic, minced
- 2 potatoes, peeled & diced
- 3 carrots, peeled & diced
- 2 celery stalks, sliced
- 1 medium onion, chopped
- Pepper
- Salt

1. Add green lentils and remaining ingredients into the slow cooker and stir well.
2. Cover and cook on high for 4 hours.
3. Stir well and serve.

**PER SERVING**

Calories 209 ;Fat 6.8 g ;Carbohydrates 30 g ;Sugar 3.2 g ;Protein 8.2g ;Cholesterol 0 mg.

# Chapter 11
## Salads

## Pepper Steak Salad

**Prep time:1-2 hours 10 minutes| Cook time:0 minutes| Serves 4**

**FOR MARINADE/DRESSING:**

- 1/4 cup balsamic vinegar
- 2 tablespoons sesame oil
- 1/2 teaspoon ground ginger
- 1 tablespoon sugar
- 1/4 teaspoon minced garlic
- 1-ounce sesame seeds
- 4 ounces leftover roast beef

**FOR SALAD:**

- 1/2-pound lettuce, shredded
- 4 ounces snow peas
- 1/2 cup carrots, sliced
- 1 cup cabbage, shredded
- 4 ounces mushrooms, sliced
- 1/2 cup red bell pepper, sliced
- 4 ounces mung bean sprouts

**TO MAKE THE MARINADE/DRESSING:**

1. Combine vinegar, sesame oil, ginger, sugar, garlic, and sesame seeds. Pour into a resalable plastic bag. Slice beef and add to marinade in the bag for 1 to 2 hours.
2. Drain, reserving liquid.

**TO MAKE THE SALAD:**

3. Toss salad ingredients, top with beef slices. Spoon remaining dressing over.

**PER SERVING**

Calories: 216 kcal, Protein: 13 g, Carbohydrates: 15 g, Fat: 13 g, Cholesterol: 25 mg, Fiber: 5 g

## Ambrosia With Coconut And Toasted Almonds

**Prep time:20 minutes| Cook time:10 minutes| Serves 8**

- 1 small, cubed pineapple (about 3 cups)
- 1/2 cup of shredded coconut; unsweetened
- 2 cored and diced red apples
- 5 segmented oranges,
- 1 peeled banana halved lengthwise and sliced crosswise.
- 1/2 cup of slivered almonds
- For Garnish: Fresh mint leaves
- 2 tablespoons of cream sherry

1. Set the oven to 325 degrees Fahrenheit. Spread the almonds out on a baking sheet and bake for 10 minutes, stirring periodically, until brown and fragrant. Immediately transfer to a platter to cool. Place coconut on the sheet and bake, often stirring, until the coconut is lightly toasted, for approximately 10 minutes. Immediately transfer to a platter to cool.
2. Combine the banana, oranges, pineapple, apples, and sherry in a large mixing bowl. Toss lightly to combine. Using separate bowls, divide the fruit mixture equally. The roasted almonds and coconut are uniformly distributed, and the mint is used as a garnish. Serve right away.

**PER SERVING**

Calories: 177 kcal, Protein: 3 g, Carbohydrates: 30 g, Fat: 5 g, Cholesterol: 0 mg, Fiber: 6 g

## Beet Walnut Salad

**Prep time:20 minutes| Cook time:0 minutes| Serves 8**

- 1/4 cup of red wine vinegar
- 1 small bunch of beets, or canned beets (no salt added) for 3 cups, drained.
- 3 tablespoons of balsamic vinegar
- 1/4 cup of chopped celery
- 1 tablespoon of olive oil
- 1/4 cup of crumbled gorgonzola cheese
- 8 cups of fresh salad greens
- 1 tablespoon of water
- 3 tablespoons of chopped walnuts
- 1/4 cup of chopped apple
- Freshly ground pepper.

1. In a saucepan, steam raw beets in water in the saucepan until soft. Skins should be slipped off. Cool by rinsing. Using a cutter, slice it into 1/2-inch rounds. Toss with red wine vinegar in a medium mixing bowl.
2. Combine the olive oil, balsamic vinegar, and water in a large mixing bowl. Toss in the salad greens.
3. Arrange salad greens on separate salad plates. Add apples, sliced beets, and celery to the top. Pepper, cheese, and walnuts are placed over the top. Serve immediately.

**PER SERVING**

Calories: 105 kcal, Protein: 3 g, Carbohydrates: 12 g, Fat: 5 g, Cholesterol: 5 mg, Fiber: 3.1 g

## Potato Salad

**Prep time:10 minutes| Cook time:0 minutes| Serves 8**

- 2 tablespoons of minced fresh dill (or 1/2 tablespoon dried)
- 1-pound potatoes, boiled and diced or steamed
- 2 ribs celery, diced (1/2 cup)
- 1 large chopped yellow onion (1 cup)
- 1/4 cup of low-calorie mayonnaise
- 1 large, diced carrot (1/2 cup)
- 1 teaspoon of ground black pepper
- 2 tablespoons of red wine vinegar
- 1 tablespoon of Dijon mustard

1. In a mixing bowl, combine all ingredients and thoroughly mix them. Before serving, chill it.

**PER SERVING**

Calories: 77 kcal, Protein: 1 g, Carbohydrates: 2 g, Fat: 1 g, Cholesterol: 2 mg, Fiber: 1.9 g

## French Green Lentil Salad

**Prep time:10 minutes| Cook time:30 minutes | Serves 6**

- 1/2 yellow finely chopped onion,
- 4 tablespoons of olive oil, divided.
- 3 minced cloves of garlic,
- 4-inch-piece of finely chopped celery stalk,
- 1 teaspoon of mustard seed
- 4-inch-piece of peeled and finely chopped carrot,
- 1 teaspoon of fennel seed
- 1/2 cup of water
- 2 cups of chicken stock or broth, vegetable stock,
- 1 bay leaf
- 1 cup of French green lentils; rinsed, picked over, then drained.
- 1/4 teaspoon of black pepper; freshly ground.
- 1 tablespoon of Dijon mustard
- 1 tablespoon of fresh chopped thyme /1 teaspoon of dried thyme
- 2 tablespoons of flat-leaf fresh (Italian) parsley, slice into strips
- 1 tablespoon of red wine vinegar or sherry vinegar

1. Two teaspoons of olive oil are heated in a large saucepan over medium heat. Add and sauté the celery, onion, and carrot for approximately 5 minutes or soften the veggies. Add and sauté the mustard seed, garlic, and fennel seed for 1 minute, or until the spices are aromatic.
2. Add the water, stock, thyme, lentils, and bay leaf. Bring the water to a boil over medium-high heat. Reduce the heat to low, partly cover, and cook for 25 to 30 minutes, or until the lentils are cooked but firm. Drain the lentils and keep the cooking liquid aside. Remove the bay leaf and transfer the lentils to a large mixing bowl.
3. Combine the mustard, vinegar, and 1/4 cup of the leftover cooking liquid in a small dish. (Any leftover liquid should be discarded or saved for subsequent use.) In a separate bowl, whisk together the remaining olive oil. Toss the lentils lightly with the parsley, vinaigrette, and pepper to coat evenly. Warm the dish before serving.

**PER SERVING**

Calories: 189 kcal, Protein: 11 g, Carbohydrates: 25 g, Fat: 5 g, Cholesterol: 2 mg, Fiber: 3.1 g

## Spinach Berry Salad

**Prep time:10 minutes| Cook time:0 minutes| Serves 4**

- 1 cup of fresh sliced strawberries
- 4 packed cups of torn fresh spinach
- 1 cup frozen or fresh blueberries
- 1/4 cup of pecan: chopped, toasted.
- 1 small sliced sweet onion,

**SALAD DRESSING:**

- 2 tablespoons of balsamic vinegar
- 1/8 teaspoon of pepper
- 2 tablespoons of honey
- 2 tablespoons of white wine vinegar or cider vinegar
- 1 teaspoon of curry powder (can be omitted)
- 2 teaspoons of Dijon mustard

1. Toss onion, spinach, blueberries, strawberries, and pecans in a large salad bowl. Combine dressing ingredients in a jar with a tight-fitting cover.
2. Shake it vigorously. Mix the salad in the dressing to coat it. Serve immediately.

**PER SERVING**

Calories: 158 kcal, Protein: 4 g, Carbohydrates: 25 g, Fat: 5 g, Cholesterol: 0 mg, Fiber: 2.3 g

## Mexican Bean Salad

**Prep time:10 minutes| Cook time:0 minutes| Serves 8**

- 2 cups cooked kidney beans
- 2 cups cooked garbanzo beans
- 1 cup tomatoes, chopped
- 3/4 cup cucumber, peeled & chopped
- 4 cups lettuce, shredded
- 1/2 cup avocado, mashed
- 2 tablespoons onion, diced
- 1/2 cup plain fat-free yogurt
- 1/4 teaspoon minced garlic
- 1/2 teaspoon cumin

1. Toss together the kidney beans, garbanzo beans, tomatoes, cucumber, and onion in a large bowl. Mix the avocado, yogurt, garlic, and cumin in a small bowl.
2. Stir the avocado mixture into the bean mixture and chill. Serve on top of shredded lettuce.

**PER SERVING**

Calories: 172 kcal, Protein: 9 g, Carbohydrates: 29 g, Fat: 3 g, Cholesterol: 0 mg, Fiber: 7 g

## Italian Eggplant Salad
**Prep time:2 hours 10 minutes| Cook time:1 ½ hour| Serves 12**

- 1 crushed clove of garlic,
- 6 eggplants
- 1 tablespoon of balsamic vinegar
- ¼ teaspoon of dried basil
- 3 tablespoons of olive oil
- 1 teaspoon of dried parsley
- 2 tablespoons of white sugar
- salt and pepper to taste.
- 1 teaspoon of dried oregano

1.  Set the oven to 350°F (180°C) (175 degrees C). Place the eggplants on a baking sheet and pierce them with a fork. Bake for at least 1 1/2 hours, or until tender, flipping halfway through. Allow cooling before peeling and dicing.
2.  Combine the olive oil, garlic, salt, vinegar, sugar, oregano, parsley, basil, and pepper in a large mixing bowl. Stir in the chopped eggplant to coat. Allow marinating for at least 2 hours before serving.

**PER SERVING**

Calories: 95 kcal, Protein: 2.4 g, Carbohydrates: 15.5 g, Fat: 3.8 g, Cholesterol: 2 mg, Fiber: 3.7 g

## Braised Celery Root
**Prep time:10 minutes| Cook time:10 minutes| Serves 6**

- 1 cup of vegetable broth or stock
- 1 peeled and diced celery root (celeriac), (about 3 cups)
- 1/4 cup of sour cream
- 1 teaspoon of Dijon mustard
- 1/4 teaspoon of salt
- 1/4 teaspoon of black pepper; freshly ground.
- 2 teaspoons of fresh thyme leaves

1.  Boil the stock in a large saucepan over high heat. Add the celery root and mix well. Reduce the heat to low when the stock resumes to a boil. Cover and cook, occasionally turning, for 10 to 12 minutes, or until the soft celery root.
2.  Shift the celery root to a bowl with a slotted spoon, cover, and keep warm. Raise the heat to be high and boil the cooking liquid in the saucepan. Cook, uncovered, for 5 minutes or until the liquid has been reduced to 1 tablespoon.
3.  Whisk in the mustard, salt, sour cream, and pepper after removing the pan from the heat. Stir in the thyme and celery root until the sauce is well cooked over medium heat. Immediately transfer to a hot serving dish and serve.

**PER SERVING**

Calories: 54 kcal, Protein: 2 g, Carbohydrates: 7 g, Fat: 2 g, Cholesterol: 4 mg, Fiber: 2.8 g

## Butternut Squash and Apple Salad
**Prep time:10 minutes| Cook time:30 minutes| Serves 6**

- 2 teaspoons of olive oil
- 1 peeled and seeded, butternut squash, 1/2-inch pieces (8 cups)
- 2 large cored and sliced apples, 1/2-inch pieces
- 1 1/2 cups of chopped celery
- 6 cups of chopped spinach,
- 2 cups of chopped carrots
- 6 cups of chopped arugula

**DRESSING:**

- 1 1/2 teaspoons of honey
- 2 teaspoons of balsamic vinegar
- 1/2 cup of plain low-fat yogurt

1.  Preheat the oven to 400 degrees Fahrenheit. Squash is tossed in olive oil and roasted for 20 to 30 minutes until golden brown and tender.
2.  Allow cooling completely. In a large mixing bowl, combine all of the veggies. Whisk together the vinegar, yogurt, and honey to make the dressing. Whisk until the mixture is completely smooth. Dress the salad with the dressing. Toss it and enjoy it.

**PER SERVING**

Calories: 215 kcal, Protein: 5 g, Carbohydrates: 42 g, Fat: 3 g, Cholesterol: 1 mg, Fiber: 4.2 g

## Yellow Pear and Cherry Tomato Salad
**Prep time:25 minutes| Cook time:0 minutes| Serves 6**

**FOR THE VINAIGRETTE**

- 1 tablespoon of minced shallot
- 1/4 teaspoon of salt
- 1 tablespoon of extra-virgin olive oil
- 1 1/2 cups of halved yellow pear tomatoes,
- 1/8 teaspoon of black pepper; freshly ground.
- 2 tablespoons of red wine vinegar or sherry vinegar
- 1 1/2 cups of halved orange cherry tomatoes,
- 4 fresh large basil leaves smash into slender ribbons.
- 1 1/2 cups of halved red cherry tomatoes

1.  To prepare the vinaigrette, mix the shallot and vinegar in a small dish and set aside for 15 minutes.
2.  Whisk in the salt, olive oil, and pepper until thoroughly combined. Toss all of the tomatoes together in a large serving bowl or salad bowl.
3.  Stir the tomatoes in the vinaigrette, add the basil and toss lightly to coat evenly. Serve immediately.

**PER SERVING**

Calories: 47 kcal, Protein: 1 g, Carbohydrates: 4 g, Fat: 3 g, Cholesterol: 0 mg, Fiber: 4.2 g

## Waldorf Salad with Yogurt
**Prep time:20 minutes| Cook time:0 minutes| Serves 4**

- 1 tablespoon of lemon juice
- 3 cored peeled and chopped tart apples.
- 1 cup of seedless grapes
- 2 tablespoons of chopped walnuts
- 2 chopped stalks of celery,
- ¼ teaspoon of celery seed
- 2 chopped green onions,
- 3 tablespoons of apple juice
- 2 tablespoons of mayonnaise
- 1 bunch of trimmed and chopped watercress
- 2 tablespoons of plain yogurt

1. Combine the lemon juice and apples in a large mixing bowl. Toss with celery, grapes, and green onions.
2. Whisk the yogurt, apple juice, grapes, and celery seeds in a small bowl. Pour over the apple mixture and gently stir. Wash and dry the watercress completely. Top with a mound of apple mixture and a sprinkling of walnuts. Arrange the greens on separate salad plates.

**PER SERVING**

Calories: 180 kcal, Protein: 3.2 g, Carbohydrates: 26.2 g, Fat: 8.7 g, Cholesterol: 3.6 mg, Fiber: 3 g

## Mandarin Almond Salad
**Prep time:20 minutes| Cook time:20 minutes| Serves 8**

- 6 thinly sliced green onions,
- 2 (11 ounces) cans of mandarin oranges, drained
- ½ cup of sliced almonds
- 2 tablespoons of white sugar
- ½ cup of olive oil
- 1 rinsed, dried, chopped head romaine lettuce -
- ¼ cup of red wine vinegar
- 1 tablespoon of white sugar
- Ground black pepper; to taste.
- ⅛ Teaspoon of red pepper flakes; crushed.

1. Combine the oranges, romaine lettuce, and green onions in a large mixing dish. In a skillet over medium heat, melt 2 tablespoons of sugar with the almonds. Cook and whisk until the sugar melts and coats the almonds. Continually stir until the nuts are light brown. Place on a platter and set aside to cool for almost 10 minutes.
2. In a jar with a tight-fitting lid, combine olive oil, red wine vinegar, red pepper flakes, one tablespoon of sugar, and black pepper. Shake well until the sugar is completely dissolved. Toss lettuce with salad dressing just before serving. Sprinkle sugared almonds on top and transfer to a nice serving dish.

**PER SERVING**

Calories: 235 kcal, Protein: 2 g, Carbohydrates: 20.2 g, Fat: 16.7 g, Cholesterol: 0 mg, Fiber: 1.8 g

## Broccoli Salad
**Prep time:45 minutes| Cook time:0 minutes| Serves 6 cups**

- ¼ cup of red onion; chopped.
- 6 cups of fresh broccoli; chopped.
- ½ cup of pumpkin seeds
- ¾ cup of dried cranberries
- ½ cup of mayonnaise
- 2 tablespoons of flax seeds
- 2 tablespoons of raspberry vinegar
- ½ cup of chopped pecans
- 2 tablespoons of white sugar

1. Toss the pumpkin seeds, broccoli, cranberries, onion, and flax seeds together in a large mixing bowl.
2. Add the vinegar, mayonnaise, and white sugar to a mixing bowl; pour over the salad. Toss to coat evenly. Allow at least 30 minutes for chilling before serving; top with pecans

**PER SERVING**

Calories: 380 kcal, Protein: 7.2 g, Carbohydrates: 29.2 g, Fat: 28.4 g, Cholesterol: 7 mg, Fiber: 2 g\

## Avocado Watermelon Salad
**Prep time:15 minutes| Cook time:0 minutes| Serves 6 cups**

- 4 cups of fresh baby spinach, torn.
- ¼ cup of walnut oil
- 4 cups of cubed watermelon
- ¼ cup of olive oil
- 2 large peeled, pitted, diced avocados -
- ½ teaspoon of sweet paprika
- 1 lime, juiced.

1. In a mixing bowl, combine the spinach, watermelon, and avocados. Combine walnut oil, lime juice, olive oil, and paprika; pour over watermelon mixture. Toss to coat evenly.

**PER SERVING**

Calories: 350 kcal, Protein: 3.2 g, Carbohydrates: 17.7 g, Fat: 32.2 g, Cholesterol: 2.6 mg, Fiber: 2 g

## Grilled Chicken Salad With Olives And Oranges

Prep time:10 minutes| Cook time:10 minutes| Serves 4

### FOR THE DRESSING:

- 4 minced garlic cloves,
- 1/2 cup of red wine vinegar
- Cracked black pepper; to taste.
- 1 tablespoon of extra-virgin olive oil
- 1 tablespoon of finely chopped celery.
- 1 tablespoon of finely chopped red onion.

### FOR THE SALAD:

- 2 garlic cloves
- 4 skinless, boneless chicken breasts, 4 ounce
- 8 cups of washed and dried leaf lettuce,
- 2 navels peeled and sliced oranges,
- 16 ripe large (black) olives

1. Whisk together the garlic, vinegar, olive oil, celery, onion, and pepper in a small bowl to prepare the dressing. Stir to ensure that everything is equally distributed. Cover and keep refrigerated until ready to use.
2. Build a fire/heat a broiler or gas grill in a charcoal grill. Spray the grill rack or broiler pan gently with cooking spray away from the heat source. Put the rack 4 to 6 inches away from the heat source. Garlic cloves should be rubbed into the chicken breasts and then discarded. For at least 5 minutes, broil or grill the chicken on each side until browned and cooked through. Allow 5 minutes for the chicken to rest on a chopping board before slicing into strips.
3. Two cups of lettuce, 1/4 of the sliced oranges, and 4 olives are placed on 4 plates. Drizzle dressing over each dish and top with 1 chicken breast sliced into strips. Serve right away.

### PER SERVING

Calories: 237 kcal, Protein: 27 g, Carbohydrates: 12 g, Fat: 9 g, Cholesterol: 49.3 mg, Fiber: 3 g

## Greek Salad

Prep time:20 minutes| Cook time:20 minutes| Serves 8

### FOR THE VINAIGRETTE:

- 2 teaspoons of fresh oregano; chopped or 3/4 teaspoon of dried oregano.
- 1 tablespoon of red wine vinegar
- 1/4 teaspoon of black pepper; freshly ground.
- 1 tablespoon of fresh lemon juice
- 2 1/2 tablespoons of olive oil; extra-virgin
- 1/4 teaspoon of salt
- For the salad:
- ½ diced red onion,
- 1 seeded and diced tomato,
- 1 large, trimmed eggplant, about 1 1/2 pounds, 1/2-inch cubes (about 7 cups)
- 2 tablespoons of pitted, black Greek olives; chopped.
- 1-pound stemmed spinach, torn into the bite-sized pieces
- 2 tablespoons of feta cheese; crumbled.
- 1 seeded unpeeled, and diced English (hothouse) cucumber,

1. Preheat the oven to 450 degrees Fahrenheit and place a rack in the bottom third. Use olive oil cooking spray lightly coat a baking sheet.
2. Mix the lemon juice, vinegar, salt, oregano, and pepper in a small bowl to create the vinaigrette. Slowly drizzle in the olive oil while whisking until emulsified. Set it aside.
3. Arrange the eggplants in a single layer on the baking sheet that has been prepared. Using olive oil frying spray, coat the eggplant and roast it for 10 minutes, then for 8 to 10 minutes longer, turn the cubes and roast until softened and gently brown. Allow cooling fully before serving.
4. Combine the cucumber, spinach, onion, tomato, and cooled eggplant in a large mixing basin. Toss the salad gently in the vinaigrette to coat evenly and thoroughly. Distribute the salad among the dishes. Toss in the feta cheese and olives. Serve right away.

### PER SERVING

Calories: 97 kcal, Protein: 3 g, Carbohydrates: 10 g, Fat: 5 g, Cholesterol: 2 mg, Fiber: 2 g

## Fattoush

**Prep time:10 minutes| Cook time:10 minutes| Serves 8**

### FOR THE DRESSING:

- 3 minced garlic cloves,
- 1/4 cup of fresh lemon juice
- 1/2 teaspoon of salt
- 1 teaspoon of ground cumin
- 1/2 teaspoon of red pepper flakes
- 1 teaspoon of ground sumac (or lemon zest to taste)
- 2 tablespoons of olive oil; extra-virgin
- 1/4 teaspoon of black pepper; freshly ground.

### FOR THE SALAD:

- 3 chopped green onions with tender green tops,
- 1 chopped head of romaine lettuce (about 4 cups)
- 1 tablespoon of chopped fresh mint.
- 2 (inches in diameter) whole-wheat pitas
- 1 seeded and diced red bell pepper,
- 2 seeded and diced tomatoes,
- 1/4 cup of fresh flat-leaf (Italian) parsley; chopped.
- 2 seeded, peeled, and diced small cucumbers

1.  Make the dressing first. In a blender or food processor, combine the garlic, lemon juice, cumin, sumac (or lemon zest), red pepper flakes, salt, and black pepper. Blend until completely smooth. Slowly drizzle in the olive oil in a fine mist while the motor is running until emulsified. Place it aside.
2.  After that, make the pita croutons. Preheat the oven to 400 degrees Fahrenheit. Rip each pita into half-inch pieces (or you may cut each into 8 triangles). Place the pieces on a baking sheet in a single layer and bake for 8 minutes, or until crisp and faintly brown. Allow cooling before serving. Now it's time to put the salad together. Toss the tomatoes, lettuce, cucumbers, green onions, mint, bell pepper, and parsley in a large mixing bowl. Toss in the dressing gently to coat evenly. Distribute the salad among the dishes. Add the croutons on top.

### PER SERVING

Calories: 108 kcal, Protein: 3 g, Carbohydrates: 15 g, Fat: 4 g, Cholesterol: 0 mg, Fiber: 3.7 g

## English Cucumber Salad with Balsamic Vinaigrette

**Prep time:15 minutes| Cook time:0 minutes | Serves 4**

- Cracked black pepper, to taste.
- 1 English cucumber washed and thinly sliced, with peel (8 to 9 inches in length),

### FOR THE DRESSING:

- 2 tablespoons of balsamic vinegar
- 1 tablespoon of fresh rosemary; finely chopped.
- 1 tablespoon of Dijon mustard
- 1 1/2 tablespoons of olive oil

1.  Combine the vinegar, rosemary, and olive oil in a small saucepan. Heat for 5 minutes over very low heat to combine and enhance the flavors. Remove the pan from the heat and whisk in the mustard until smooth.
2.  Place the cucumber slices in a serving dish. Toss the cucumbers in the dressing to evenly coat them. Toss in a pinch of black pepper to taste. Place in the refrigerator until ready to serve.

### PER SERVING

Calories: 67 kcal, Protein: 0.5 g, Carbohydrates: 5 g, Fat: 5 g, Cholesterol: 0 mg, Fiber: 1 g

## Couscous Salad

**Prep time:10 minutes| Cook time:0 minutes| Serves 8**

- 1/2 teaspoon of ground black pepper
- 1 red medium bell pepper, 1/4-inch pieces
- 1 cup of zucchini, 1/4-inch pieces
- 1/2 cup of red onion; finely chopped.
- 3/4 teaspoon of ground cumin
- 1 cup of whole-wheat couscous
- 2 tablespoons of olive oil; extra virgin
- Chopped fresh basil, parsley, or oregano for garnish (optional)
- 1 tablespoon of lemon juice

1.  Cook the couscous according to the package's directions. When the couscous is done, fluff it up with a fork. Add bell pepper, zucchini, cumin, onion, and black pepper. Put it aside.
2.  Whisk together the lemon juice and olive oil in a small bowl. Toss the couscous mixture to mix. Cover and store in the refrigerator. Chill before serving. Fresh herbs may be used as a garnish.

### PER SERVING

Calories: 136 kcal, Protein: 4 g, Carbohydrates: 21 g, Fat: 4 g, Cholesterol: trace, Fiber: 7 g

## Artichokes Alla Romana

**Prep time:15 minutes| Cook time:50 minutes| Serves 8**

- 1 tablespoon of olive oil
- 2 cups of fresh whole-wheat breadcrumbs,
- 1 teaspoon of fresh oregano; chopped.
- 4 artichokes; large globe
- 1/3 cup of grated Parmesan cheese
- 2 halved lemons,
- 1 cup of dry white wine
- 3 finely chopped garlic cloves,
- 1 tablespoon of grated lemon zest
- 2 tablespoons of fresh flat-leaf finely chopped (Italian) parsley.
- 1 cup and 2 to 4 tablespoons of low-sodium chicken stock or vegetable
- 1 tablespoon of minced shallot
- 1/4 teaspoon of black pepper; freshly ground.

1. Set the oven to 400 degrees Fahrenheit. Combine the olive oil and breadcrumbs in a mixing dish. Toss to coat evenly. Place the crumbs in a baking pan bake it until gently brown for approximately 10 minutes, stirring once halfway through. Allow cooling before serving.
2. Snip off tough outer leaves and cut the stem flush with the base, one artichoke at a time. The top third of the leaves are cut off with a serrated knife, and scissors remove any remaining thorns. To avoid discoloration, rub the sliced edges with half of a lemon. Remove the tiny leaves from the middle and separate the inner leaves. Scoop out the fuzzy choke using a spoon or melon baller, then pour some lemon juice into the hollow. Trim the rest of the artichokes the same way.
3. Stir the breadcrumbs with parsley, Parmesan, lemon zest, garlic, and pepper in a large mixing bowl. Add the 2 to 4 tbsp. of stock, only 1 tbsp. at a time, until the stuffing begins to cling together in tiny clumps.
4. Make a small mound in the middle of the artichokes with 2/3 of the filling. Spread the leaves wide, beginning at the bottom, and spoon a rounded spoonful of filling at the base of each leaf. (You may prepare the artichokes up to this stage ahead of time and keep them refrigerated.)
5. Combine shallot, wine, 1 cup stock, and oregano in a Dutch oven with a tight-fitting lid. (Note: If you cook the artichokes in cast iron, they will become brown.) Boil it, then turn off the heat. Arrange the artichokes in a single layer in the liquid, stems down. Cover and cook for 45 minutes, or until the outer leaves are soft (add water if necessary). Place the artichokes on a cooling rack to cool gently. Each artichoke should be quartered and served warm.

**PER SERVING**

Calories: 123 kcal, Protein: 6 g, Carbohydrates: 18 g, Fat: 3 g, Cholesterol: 3 mg, Fiber: 4.2 g

## Apple-Fennel Slaw

**Prep time:15 minutes| Cook time:0 minutes| Serves 4**

- 2 grated carrots,
- 1 medium-sized thinly sliced fennel bulb
- 2 tablespoons of raisins
- 1 large thinly sliced and cored Granny Smith apple,
- 4 lettuce leaves
- 1/2 cup of apple juice
- 1 tablespoon of olive oil
- 2 tablespoons of apple cider vinegar
- 1 teaspoon of sugar

1. Put the carrots, apple, fennel, and raisins in a large mixing bowl to prepare the slaw. Sprinkle with olive oil, cover, and chill while preparing the rest of the ingredients.
2. Combine the apple juice and sugar in a small saucepan. Cook, occasionally stirring until the liquid has been reduced to about 1/4 cup, approximately 10 minutes. Remove from the heat and set aside to cool. Add the apple cider vinegar and mix well. Pour the apple juice mixture over the slaw and toss to blend thoroughly.
3. Allow cooling completely. Serve with lettuce leaves on the side.

**PER SERVING**

Calories: 124 kcal, Protein: 2 g, Carbohydrates: 22 g, Fat: 4 g, Cholesterol: 0 mg, Fiber: 4 g\

## Salmon Salad

**Prep time:10 minutes| Cook time:0 minutes| Serves 4**

- 1 diced white onion,
- 1-pound broiled salmon fillet,
- 1 cup of chopped spinach,
- 1 cup of chopped lettuce,
- 1 tablespoon of lemon juice
- 1 teaspoon of ground paprika
- 1 teaspoon of olive oil

1. Combine the onion, spinach, lettuce, salmon fillet, and paprika in a salad bowl. Shake the ingredients vigorously. The salad should then be drizzled with lemon juice and olive oil.

**PER SERVING**

Calories: 177 kcal, Protein: 22.7 g, Carbohydrates: 3.6 g, Fat: 8.4 g, Cholesterol: 20 mg, Fiber: 1.1 g

## Grilled Vegetable Orzo Salad

**Prep time:10 minutes| Cook time:20 minutes| Serves 8**

- 1 cup zucchini, cut into 1-inch (2.5-cm) cubes
- 1/2 cup red bell pepper, cut into 1-inch (2.5-cm) cubes
- 1/2 cup yellow bell pepper, cut into 1-inch (2.5-cm) cubes
- 1 cup red onion, cut into 1-inch (2.5-cm) cubes
- 1/2 teaspoon minced garlic
- 3 tablespoons olive oil, divided
- 1 teaspoon freshly ground black pepper, divided
- 8 ounce orzo
- 1/3 cup lemon juice
- 1/4 cup pine nuts, toasted

1. Prepare the grill. Toss zucchini, bell peppers, onion, and garlic with 1 tablespoon olive oil and 1/2 teaspoon pepper in a large bowl. Transfer to a grill basket. Grill for 15 to 20 minutes, or until browned, stirring occasionally. Meanwhile, cook the orzo according to package directions. Drain and transfer to a large serving bowl.
2. Add the roasted vegetables to the pasta. Combine the lemon juice and remaining olive oil and pepper and pour on the pasta and vegetables. Let cool to room temperature. Stir in the pine nuts.

**PER SERVING**

Calories: 201 kcal, Protein: 5 g, Carbohydrates: 27 g, Fat: 9 g, Cholesterol: 0 mg, Fiber: 2 g

## Tofu Salad

**Prep time:10 minutes| Cook time:0 minutes| Serves 6**

**FOR SALAD:**
- 1/2-pound lettuce, shredded
- 4 ounces snow peas
- 1/2 cup carrot, shredded
- 1 cup cabbage, shredded
- 1/2 cup mushrooms, sliced
- 1/2 cup red bell pepper, sliced
- 4 ounces' mung bean sprouts
- 1/2 cup tomato, sliced
- 12 ounces tofu, drained and cubed

**FOR DRESSING:**
- 1 tablespoon rice vinegar
- 2 tablespoons sesame oil
- 3 tablespoons Reduced-Sodium Soy Sauce
- 2 cloves garlic, crushed
- 1 tablespoon sesame seeds
- 1/2 teaspoon ground ginger

1. To make the salad: Toss salad ingredients.
2. To make the dressing: Combine dressing ingredients and spoon dressing over salad.

**PER SERVING**

Calories: 111 kcal, Protein: 5 g, Carbohydrates: 57 g, Fat: 6 g, Cholesterol: 0 mg, Fiber: 3 g

## Fruited Pistachios Millet Salad

**Prep time:10 minutes| Cook time:15 minutes| Serves 4**

- 1 cup millet
- ½ cup pistachios, toasted
- ½ cup dried longings
- ½ cup peanuts, toasted
- 2 kiwifruits, diced
- Zest and juice of 2 orange
- 3 tbsps. ruby port
- 2 tbsps. finely chopped turmeric

1. Bring 2 quarts of lightly salted water to a boil over high heat and pour the millet. Return to a boil, lower the heat to medium, cover, and simmer for 12 to 14 minutes. Drain off the water, rinse millet until cool, set aside.
2. Whisk the orange juice, zest, and ruby port in a large bowl. Toss until well combined. Stir in the pistachios, longings, peanuts, kiwifruit, and turmeric and toss until well combined. Put in the cooked millet and toss to blend. Refrigerate before serving.

**PER SERVING**

Calories: 388 kcal, Protein: 7.8 g, Carbohydrates: 87.2 g, Fat: 31.3 g, Cholesterol: 0 mg, Fiber: 8.3 g

## Lemony Kale Salad

**Prep time:10 minutes| Cook time:10 minutes| Serves 4**

- 2 heads kale
- Sea salt and freshly ground pepper
- Juice of 1 lemon
- 1 tbsp. olive oil
- 2 cloves garlic, minced
- 1 cup cherry tomatoes, sliced

1. Wash and dry kale. Tear the kale into small pieces. Heat olive oil in a large skillet and add the garlic. Cook for 1 minute and then add the kale.
2. Add the tomatoes after kale wilted. Cook until tomatoes are softened, then remove from heat. Put tomatoes and kale together in a bowl, and season with sea salt and freshly ground pepper. Drizzle with remaining olive oil and lemon juice, serve.

**PER SERVING**

Calories: 59 kcal, Protein: 2 g, Carbohydrates: 5.95 g, Fat: 3.83g, Cholesterol: 0 mg, Fiber: 1.9 g.

# Chapter 12
# Sandwiches, Rolls, and Wraps

## Tofu and Cucumber Spring Rolls

**Prep time: 10 minutes | Cook time: 20 minutes | Makes 5 Rolls**

- ⅓ cup Tangy Soy Sauce
- 3 tablespoons nut butter (almond, cashew, or all-natural peanut butter)
- 6 ounces firm tofu, cut into 10 (½-inch wide) strips
- 5 rehydrated rice paper wraps
- 1 cucumber, peeled and cut into sticks

1. Preheat the oven to 425°F. Line a baking sheet with parchment paper and set aside.
2. In a small bowl, mix the Tangy Soy Sauce and the nut butter until well blended.
3. Drizzle 2 to 3 tablespoons of the sauce mixture over the tofu strips. You'll have some sauce left over. You can use this for dipping.
4. Place the tofu strips on the prepared baking sheet and bake for 20 minutes.
5. Place the rehydrated rice paper wraps on a flat surface.
6. Once the tofu is done cooking, place two strips of tofu and a few cucumber sticks in the center of one wrap.
7. Fold the sides of the rice paper over the filling, then tightly roll from the bottom up all the way until the wrap is sealed. Repeat with the other wraps.
8. Enjoy the spring rolls with the dipping sauce.

**PER SERVING (1 ROLL)**

Calories: 181; Total fat: 8g; Saturated fat: 1g; Trans fat: 0g; Protein: 9g; Total carbohydrate: 20g; Fiber: 2g; Sodium: 255mg; Potassium: 192mg

## Spicy Chickpea and Cilantro Wrap

**Prep time: 15 minutes | Serves 4**

- 2 (15-ounce) cans low-sodium chickpeas, drained and rinsed
- ½ cup minced fresh cilantro
- ⅓ cup Spicy Honey Sauce
- 1 cup low-fat Greek yogurt
- 5 (6½-inch) whole wheat or whole-grain pitas, cut open at the top

1. In a blender, place the chickpeas, cilantro, and Spicy Honey Sauce and blend until smooth.
2. Scoop ¾ cup of the chickpea mixture and 3 tablespoons of yogurt into each pita. Serve immediately.

**PER SERVING (1 PITA)**

Calories: 310; Total fat: 10g; Saturated fat: 1g; Trans fat: 0g; Protein: 12g; Total carbohydrate: 47g; Fiber: 9g; Sodium: 632mg; Potassium: 311mg

## Egg White and Avocado Breakfast Wrap

**Prep time: 10 minutes | Cook time: 6 minutes | Serves 1**

- 2 teaspoons olive oil
- ½ red pepper, seeded and sliced
- ½ cup liquid egg whites
- ¼ avocado, pitted and sliced
- 2 tablespoons fresh lime salsa
- 1 (6½-inch) whole wheat tortilla (or pita)

1. In a medium skillet, heat the olive oil over medium-high heat. Add the red pepper and cook for 3 minutes until slightly soft, then remove and set aside.
2. In the same skillet over medium-high heat, scramble the egg whites until cooked through and no longer runny, about 3 minutes, then remove from heat.
3. Spread the scrambled eggs, cooked red peppers, avocado, and Fresh Lime Salsa over the tortilla.
4. Wrap up the tortilla and serve immediately.

**PER SERVING (1 PITA)**

Calories: 407; Total fat: 21g; Saturated fat: 5g; Trans fat: 0g; Protein: 22g; Total carbohydrate: 37g; Fiber: 12g; Sodium: 488mg; Potassium: 1,099mg

## Tuna-Carrot Rice Balls

**Prep time: 25 minutes | Cook time: 35 minutes | Serves 1**

- ¼ cup short-grain brown rice, rinsed
- ¾ cup water, divided
- ½ cup diced carrots
- 1 (2½-ounce) can low-sodium tuna packed in water, drained
- ½ teaspoon sesame oil
- Sea salt
- Freshly ground black pepper
- 2 (4-by-5-inch) sheets dried seaweed

1. Combine the rice and ½ cup water in a medium saucepan over high heat and bring to a boil. Cover, reduce the heat to low, and simmer until the liquid is absorbed, about 30 minutes. Remove from the heat, fluff with a fork, and let cool slightly.
2. Place the carrots and the remaining ¼ cup water in a medium skillet over medium heat and cook until the carrots soften, about 3 minutes. Remove the skillet from the heat.
3. Add the tuna, sesame oil, salt, and pepper to the skillet and mix thoroughly.
4. Place the cooked rice in a medium bowl and stir in the tuna mixture.
5. Wet your hands with water and shape the mixture into 2 separate rice balls.
6. Wrap 1 sheet of seaweed around each rice ball and serve.

**PER SERVING (2 BALLS)**

Calories: 158; Total fat: 2g; Saturated fat: 0g; Trans fat: 0g; Protein: 10g; Total carbohydrate: 24g; Fiber: 2g; Sodium: 224mg; Potassium: 218mg

## Seaweed Rice Rolls
**Prep time: 45 minutes | Serves 2**

- ¾ cup short-grain brown rice, rinsed
- 1½ cups water
- 1 (4-ounce) can low-sodium tuna packed in water, drained
- ½ tablespoon sesame oil
- Sea salt
- Freshly ground black pepper
- 2 (7-by-8-inch) sheets dried seaweed
- 2 cups sesame spinach

1. In a medium saucepan over high heat, combine the rice and the water and bring to a boil. Cover, reduce the heat to low, and simmer until the liquid is absorbed, about 30 minutes. Remove from the heat, fluff with a fork, and let cool.
2. In a small bowl, mix the tuna and sesame oil, and season with salt and pepper.
3. Place the seaweed sheets on a flat surface and evenly spread ¾ cup of the rice on one sheet.
4. Place half the tuna mixture and half the Sesame Spinach on the rice along one end of the seaweed.
5. Slowly roll up the seaweed rice wrap, starting at the end with the tuna and spinach, and gently press down to make a firm roll. Make sure to apply firm, even pressure over the entire roll when rolling.
6. Wet the end of the seaweed wrap with water to seal the roll. Repeat to make the other roll.
7. Cut the rolls into equal slices and enjoy immediately.

**PER SERVING (1 ROLL)**

Calories: 481; Total fat: 14g; Saturated fat: 3g; Trans fat: 0g; Protein: 24g; Total carbohydrate: 68g; Fiber: 7g; Sodium: 498mg; Potassium: 1,312mg

## Spicy Salmon Avocado Sandwich
**Prep time: 10 minutes | Serves 4**

- 2 (7½-ounce) cans low-sodium, deboned salmon packed in water, drained
- ⅓ cup Spicy Honey Sauce
- 3 tablespoons low-fat plain Greek yogurt
- 5 slices whole wheat or whole-grain toast
- 1 avocado, thinly sliced

1. In a medium bowl, mix the salmon, Spicy Honey Sauce, and Greek yogurt until well combined.
2. Scoop about 5 tablespoons of the spicy salmon mixture onto each toast slice and top with avocado slices for an open-faced sandwich. Serve immediately.

**PER SERVING (1 OPEN-FACED SANDWICH)**

Calories: 354; Total fat: 18g; Saturated fat: 2g; Trans fat: 0g; Protein: 25g; Total carbohydrate: 26g; Fiber: 6g; Sodium: 479mg; Potassium: 587mg

## Fish Tacos
**Prep time: 5 minutes | Cook time: 20 minutes | Serves 4**

- 1 pound white fish (such as tilapia), cut into bite-size pieces
- 1 tablespoon olive oil
- Sea salt
- Freshly ground black pepper
- 1 cup low-fat plain Greek yogurt
- 5 (6½-inch) whole wheat or whole-grain corn tortillas
- 2½ cups shredded romaine lettuce
- 2 tablespoons freshly squeezed lime juice

1. Preheat the oven to 375°F. Line a baking sheet with parchment paper.
2. Season the fish with the olive oil, salt, and pepper. Place the fish on the prepared baking sheet and bake for 20 minutes, until slightly golden brown.
3. While the fish is cooking, in a small bowl, combine the yogurt with another pinch of salt and pepper.
4. Once the fish is cooked, place  of the fish in a tortilla with ½ cup romaine, 1 teaspoon lime juice, and a dollop of yogurt. Repeat with the remaining tortillas and serve immediately.

**PER SERVING (1 TACO)**

Calories: 272; Total fat: 7g; Saturated fat: 2g; Trans fat: 0g; Protein: 23g; Total carbohydrate: 29g; Fiber: 2g; Sodium: 450mg; Potassium: 623mg

## Lemon-Garlic Tuna Sandwich
**Prep time: 15 minutes | Serves 5**

- 3 (4-ounce) cans low-sodium tuna packed in water, drained
- 1 tablespoon Lemon-Garlic Sauce
- 3 celery stalks, diced
- ½ cup low-fat plain Greek yogurt
- 2 (12-inch) whole wheat or whole-grain baguette loaves

1. In a large bowl, combine the tuna, Lemon-Garlic Sauce, and celery until well mixed. Stir in the yogurt.
2. Scoop half of the tuna salad onto each baguette and serve immediately.

**PER SERVING (SANDWICH)**

Calories: 353; Total Fat: 7g; Saturated fat: 2g; Trans fat: 0g; Protein: 23g; Total Carbohydrate: 44g; Fiber: 7g; Sodium: 603mg; Potassium: 457mg

## Bright Lemon-Cucumber Chicken Rolls

**Prep time: 10 minutes | Cook time: 20 minutes | Makes 10 Rolls**

- 1 pound boneless, skinless chicken breast
- 5 cups water
- 1 cup low-fat plain Greek yogurt
- ¾ cup diced cucumber
- 1 tablespoon freshly squeezed lemon juice
- Sea salt
- Freshly ground black pepper
- 10 slices whole wheat or whole-grain bread

1. In a large skillet, cover the chicken with the water and poach for 20 minutes over medium-high heat.
2. Remove the chicken from the water, let it cool, and shred it using two forks.
3. In a medium bowl, mix the chicken, yogurt, cucumber, and lemon juice, and season with salt and pepper.
4. Place the bread on a flat surface and use a rolling pin or your hands to flatten it out. Cut the crusts off with a knife.
5. Evenly divide the chicken mixture between the flattened bread slices and roll them up tightly. Enjoy immediately.

**PER SERVING (1 ROLL)**

Calories: 143; Total fat: 2g; Saturated fat: 1g; Trans fat: 0g; Protein: 15g; Total carbohydrate: 15g; Fiber: 2g; Sodium: 179mg; Potassium: 268mg

## Chicken Pesto Baguette

**Prep time: 10 minutes | Cook time: 20 minutes | Serves 6**

- 1 pound boneless, skinless chicken breast
- 5 cups water
- 1 cup low-fat plain Greek yogurt
- 1½ cups spinach and walnut pesto
- 2½ cups arugula
- 2 (12-inch) whole wheat or whole-grain baguettes, halved lengthwise

1. In a large skillet, cover the chicken with the water and poach for 20 minutes over medium-high heat.
2. Remove the chicken from the water, let it cool, and finely dice the chicken.
3. In a large bowl, mix the diced chicken, yogurt, and Spinach and Walnut Pesto until combined.
4. Arrange the arugula on the baguettes and evenly divide the chicken salad between them. Slice each baguette into three equal parts. Serve immediately.

**PER SERVING (SANDWICH)**

Calories: 527; Total fat: 33g; Saturated fat: 5g; Trans fat: 0g; Protein: 31g; Total carbohydrate: 26g; Fiber: 5g; Sodium: 499mg; Potassium: 617mg

## Chicken Pita Wraps with Oregano-Thyme Sauce

**Prep time: 5 minutes, plus 30 minutes to marinate | Cook time: 25 minutes | Serves 4**

- 1 pound skinless, boneless chicken thighs
- ¼ cup Oregano-Thyme Sauce
- 1 cucumber
- 1 cup low-fat plain Greek yogurt
- Sea salt
- Freshly ground black pepper
- 5 (6½-inch) whole wheat or whole-grain pitas

1. Place the chicken and Oregano-Thyme Sauce into a large resealable plastic bag and marinate the chicken in the refrigerator for 30 minutes or overnight.
2. Preheat the oven to 425°F. Line a baking sheet with parchment paper.
3. Place the chicken on the prepared baking sheet and bake for 25 minutes until the internal temperature is 165°F.
4. While the chicken is cooking, mince and measure out ½ cup of the cucumber and cut the rest into strips.
5. In a small bowl, mix the minced cucumber and Greek yogurt and season with salt and pepper.
6. Once the chicken is done cooking, cut it into ½-inch strips.
7. Evenly divide the chicken, cucumber strips, and yogurt sauce in the middle of the pitas, fold them over, and serve.

**PER SERVING (1 PITA)**

Calories: 258; Total fat: 8g; Saturated fat: 2g; Trans fat: 0g; Protein: 24g; Total carbohydrate: 23g; Fiber: 2g; Sodium: 446mg; Potassium: 495mg

## Lean Beef Lettuce Wraps

**Prep time: 5 minutes | Cook time: 15 minutes | Serves 4**

- 1 pound lean ground beef
- ½ white onion, diced
- ⅓ cup honey-garlic sauce
- 1 tablespoon white vinegar
- 10 large lettuce leaves, washed and dried

1. In a large skillet over high heat, cook the ground beef for 10 minutes until browned. Drain the fat.
2. Add the onion, Honey-Garlic Sauce, and vinegar to the pan, and cook an additional 3 to 5 minutes. Evenly divide the beef mixture between the lettuce leaves and fold them over. Enjoy immediately.

**PER SERVING (1 WRAP)**

Calories: 172; Total fat: 7g; Saturated fat: 2g; Trans fat: 0g; Protein: 21g; Total carbohydrate: 8g; Fiber: 1g; Sodium: 577mg; Potassium: 99mg

## Turkey Sloppy Joes

**Prep time: 5 minutes | Cook time: 20 minutes | Serves 4**

- 1 tablespoon olive oil
- ½ white onion, diced
- 1 red bell pepper, diced
- 1 pound ground turkey
- 1 cup tasty tomato sauce
- 5 whole wheat or whole-grain burger buns

1. In a medium skillet over high heat, heat the olive oil and sauté the onion and bell pepper for 3 to 5 minutes. Transfer the vegetables from the pan to a small bowl and set aside.
2. Add the ground turkey to the pan and cook over high heat until there is no pink left, about 5 minutes.
3. Add the vegetables and the Tasty Tomato Sauce to the pan, reduce the heat to medium, and simmer for 10 minutes.
4. Scoop the mixture onto the burger buns and enjoy immediately.

**PER SERVING (1 SANDWICH)**

Calories: 380; Total fat: 14g; Saturated fat: 3g; Trans fat: 0g; Protein: 21g; Total carbohydrate: 48g; Fiber: 0g; Sodium: 284mg; Potassium: 467mg

## Greek Pizza

**Prep time: 15 minutes | Cook time: 25 minutes | Serves 4**

- 1½ cups whole wheat or whole-grain self-rising flour, plus more for dusting
- 1 cup low-fat plain Greek yogurt
- 1½ cups spinach and walnut pesto
- 1 tomato, thinly sliced
- ½ cup thinly sliced white mushrooms

1. Preheat the oven to 350°F. Line a baking sheet with parchment paper.
2. In a medium bowl, place the flour. Mix in the yogurt ¼ cup at a time until the dough is smooth. Knead it into a ball.
3. Sprinkle 1 or 2 tablespoons of flour onto a cutting board or hard, clean surface, and form the dough ball into a 12-inch circle.
4. Transfer the dough to the baking sheet and spread it evenly with the Spinach and Walnut Pesto.
5. Arrange the tomato and mushrooms on top of the sauce.
6. Bake the pizza for 25 minutes, until the crust is golden brown. Enjoy immediately.

**PER SERVING (PIZZA)**

Calories: 433; Total fat: 31g; Saturated fat: 5g; Trans fat: 0g; Protein: 10g; Total carbohydrate: 33g; Fiber: 5g; Sodium: 279mg; Potassium: 443mg

## Spinach, Walnut, and Black Bean Burgers

**Prep time: 10 minutes | Cook time: 20 minutes | Makes 6 Patties**

- 1 tablespoon olive oil
- 1 white onion, diced
- 1 cup spinach and walnut pesto
- 2 (19-ounce) cans low-sodium black beans, drained and rinsed
- 2 large eggs
- ½ cup whole wheat or whole-grain bread crumbs

1. Preheat the oven to 375°F. Line a baking sheet with parchment paper.
2. In a medium skillet, heat the olive oil over high heat and sauté the onion until translucent, about 3 minutes.
3. Put the onion, Spinach and Walnut Pesto, beans, eggs, and bread crumbs to a blender or food processor and pulse until combined.
4. Using a ½-cup scoop, form 6 patties and place them on the prepared baking sheet.
5. Bake the patties in the oven for 20 minutes. Enjoy immediately.

**PER SERVING (1 BURGER)**

Calories: 383; Total fat: 24g; Saturated fat: 4g; Trans fat: 0g; Protein: 12g; Total carbohydrate: 32g; Fiber: 9g; Sodium: 253mg; Potassium: 461mg

## Old Bay Crispy Kale Chips

**Prep time:10 minutes| Cook time:25 minutes| Serves 4**

- bunch kale, washed
- tablespoons olive oil
- 1 to 3 teaspoons Old Bay Seasoning
- Sea salt, to taste

1. Preheat the oven to 300 Remove the kale's tough stems and shred the leaves into large pieces. Combine all of the ingredients in a large mixing bowl. Toss with olive oil and spices to coat. Arrange the leaves on prepared baking sheets in a single layer.
2. Bake for 10 minutes, uncovered, before rotating pans. Bake for a further 15 minutes, or until crisp and beginning to brown. Allow at least 5 minutes to stand before serving.

**PER SERVING**

Calories: 101 kcal, Protein: 3 g, Carbohydrates: 8 g, Fat: 7 g, Cholesterol: 0 mg, Fiber: 2 g

## Nutty Broccoli Slaw

**Prep time:15 minutes| Cook time:0 minutes|Serves 16**

- 2 cups of sliced green onions: 2 bunches
- package of chicken ramen noodles (3 ounces)
- 1-1/2 cups of broccoli florets
- 1 package of broccoli coleslaw mix; (16 ounces)
- 1 can of ripe olives (6 ounces); drained and halved
- 1 cup of sunflower kernels, toasted
- 1/2 cup of slivered almonds, toasted
- 1/2 cup cider vinegar
- 1/2 cup of sugar
- 1/2 cup olive oil

1. Open the noodle seasoning package and put the crushed noodles in a large mixing bowl. Combine the onions, sunflower kernels, broccoli, slaw mix, olives, and almonds.
2. Combine the seasoning package's oil, vinegar, sugar, and contents in a jar with a tight-fitting cover; shake thoroughly. Drizzle the dressing over salad and toss to combine. Serve right away.

**PER SERVING**

Calories: 206 kcal, Protein: 4 g, Carbohydrates: 16 g, Fat: 15 g, Cholesterol: 0 mg, Fiber: 3 g

## Chipotle Lime Avocado Salad

**Prep time:15 minutes| Cook time:0 minutes| Serves 4**

- 1/4 cup lime juice
- 1/4 cup of maple syrup
- 1/2 teaspoon chipotle pepper, ground
- 1/4 teaspoon cayenne pepper
- 2 peeled and sliced medium ripe avocados
- peeled and sliced 1/2 a medium cucumber
- a tablespoon fresh chives, minced
- large tomatoes, peeled and cut into 1/2-inch thick slices

1. Whisk lime juice, maple syrup, chipotle pepper, and, if preferred, cayenne pepper together in a small bowl until well combined.
2. Combine avocados, cucumber, and chives in a separate bowl. Drizzle dressing over the salad and gently mix to coat. Serve with tomatoes on the side.

**PER SERVING**

Calories: 191 kcal, Protein: 3 g, Carbohydrates: 25 g, Fat: 11 g, Cholesterol: 0 mg, Fiber: 6 g

## Nuts And Seeds Trail Mix

**Prep time:5 minutes| Cook time:0 minutes| Serves 5 cups**

- 1 cup salted pumpkin seeds or petites
- 1 cup unbranched almonds
- 1 cup unsalted sunflower kernels
- 1 cup walnut halves
- 1 cup dried apricots
- 1 cup dark chocolate chips

1. Place all ingredients in a large bowl; toss to combine. Store in an airtight container.

**PER SERVING**

Calories: 336 kcal, Protein: 11 g, Carbohydrates: 22 g, Fat: 25 g, Cholesterol: 0 mg, Fiber: 4 g

## Hummus

**Prep time:25 minutes| Cook time:20 minutes plus chilling | Serves 1 1/2 cup**

- 1/4 cup of fresh lemon juice
- 1/2 teaspoon of baking soda
- 1/2 teaspoon of kosher salt
- can (15 ounces) garbanzo beans/chickpeas: rinsed & drained
- 1 tablespoon of minced garlic
- 1/2 cup of tahini
- 1/2 teaspoon of ground cumin
- tablespoons of extra virgin olive oil
- Optional: roasted garbanzo beans, Olive oil, ground sumac, toasted sesame seeds,
- 1/4 cup of cold water

1. Place the garbanzo beans and enough water to cover them by 1 inch in a large saucepan. Rub the beans together gently to release the outer skin. Pour off the water as well as any floating skins. Drain after repeating steps 2-3 times unless no skins float to the top. Return to saucepan; stir in baking soda and 1 inch of water. Bring to a boil, then turn off the heat. Cook, uncovered, for 20-25 minutes, or until beans are soft and begin to come apart.
2. Meanwhile, puree the garlic, lemon juice, and salt in a blender until smooth. Allow 10 minutes to stand before straining and discarding the solids. Cumin is added at this point. Combine tahini and olive oil in a small bowl.
3. Blend the beans with the cold water in a blender. Cover loosely with cover and process until absolutely smooth. Stir in the lemon mixture in the food processor. Slowly drizzle in the tahini mixture while the blender runs, scraping down the sides as required. If desired, add more salt and cumin to the seasoning. Refrigerate for at least 30 minutes after transferring the mixture to the serving bowl. Additional toppings or olive oil may be added if desired.

**PER SERVING**

Calories: 250 kcal, Protein: 7 g, Carbohydrates: 15 g, Fat: 19 g, Cholesterol: 0 mg, Fiber: 5 g

## Honey-Lime Berry Salad

**Prep time:15 minutes| Cook time:0 minutes| Serves 10**

- 4 cups fresh strawberries, halved
- cups fresh blueberries
- medium Granny Smith apples, cubed
- 1/3 cup lime juice
- 1/4 to 1/3 cup honey
- 2 tablespoons minced fresh mint

1. Combine strawberries, blueberries, and apples in a large mixing dish. Combine the lime juice, honey, and mint in a small mixing bowl. Toss the fruit in the dressing to coat.

**PER SERVING**

Calories: 93 kcal, Protein: 1 g, Carbohydrates: 24 g, Fat: 0 g, Cholesterol: 0 mg, Fiber: 3 g

## Smoky Cauliflower

**Prep time:30 minutes| Cook time:0 minutes| Serves 8**

- 1 tablespoons of olive oil
- 1 large head cauliflower: 1-inch florets: about 9 cups
- 3/4 teaspoon of salt
- 1 teaspoon of smoked paprika
- tablespoons of minced fresh parsley
- 2 garlic cloves: minced

1. In a large mixing bowl, place the cauliflower. Combine the oil, paprika, and salt. Drizzle the dressing over the cauliflower and toss to coat. Fill a 15x10x1-inch baking pan halfway with the batter.
2. Bake for 10 minutes at 450°F, uncovered. Add the garlic and mix well. Bake for another 10-15 minutes, stirring periodically, or until cauliflower is soft and lightly browned. Serve with a parsley garnish.

**PER SERVING**

Calories: 58 kcal, Protein: 2 g, Carbohydrates: 6 g, Fat: 4 g, Cholesterol: 0 mg, Fiber: 3 g

## Chewy Granola Bars

**Prep time:10 minutes| Cook time:25 minutes plus cooling| Serves 2 dozen**

- 1/2 cup butter, softened
- 1 cup packed brown sugar
- 1/4 cup sugar
- 1 large egg, room temperature
- tablespoons honey
- 1/2 teaspoon vanilla extract
- 1 cup all-purpose flour
- 1 teaspoon ground cinnamon
- 1/2 teaspoon baking powder
- 1/4 teaspoon salt
- 1-1/2 cups quick-cooking oats
- 1-1/4 cups rice krispies
- 1 cup chopped nuts
- Optional: Raisins or semisweet chocolate chips (1 cup each)

1. Preheat oven to 350°F. Cream butter and sugars until light and fluffy, 5-7 minutes. Beat in egg, honey, and vanilla.
2. Whisk together flour, cinnamon, baking powder, and salt; gradually beat into creamed mixture.
3. Stir in oats, Rice Krispies, nuts, raisins, or chocolate chips. Press into a greased 13x9-in. pan. Bake until light brown, 25-30 minutes. Cool on a wire rack. Cut into bars.

**PER SERVING**

Calories: 160 kcal, Protein: 3 g, Carbohydrates: 22 g, Fat: 7 g, Cholesterol: 19 mg, Fiber: 1 g

## Mango Black Bean Salsa

**Prep time:15 minutes| Cook time:0 minutes | Serves 12**

- 1 can (15 ounces) black beans, rinsed and drained
- 1 medium mango, peeled and cubed
- 1/4 cup finely chopped onion
- 1/4 cup minced fresh cilantro
- tablespoons lime juice
- 1 teaspoon garlic salt
- 1/4 teaspoon ground cumin
- Baked tortilla chip scoops

1. In a large bowl, mix all ingredients except chips. Refrigerate until serving. Serve with chips.

**PER SERVING**

Calories: 70 kcal, Protein: 3 g, Carbohydrates: 14 g, Fat: 0 g, Cholesterol: 0 mg, Fiber: 2 g

## Homemade Guacamole

**Prep time:10 minutes| Cook time:0 minutes| Serves 2 cups**

- 1 medium ripe avocados, peeled and cubed
- 1 garlic clove, minced
- 1/4 to 1/2 teaspoon salt
- 1 small onion, finely chopped
- 1 to 2 tablespoons lime juice
- 1 tablespoon minced fresh cilantro
- medium tomatoes, seeded and chopped, optional
- 1/4 cup mayonnaise, optional

1. Mash avocados with garlic and salt. Stir in remaining ingredients, adding tomatoes and mayonnaise if desired.

**PER SERVING**

Calories: 90 kcal, Protein: 1 g, Carbohydrates: 6 g, Fat: 8 g, Cholesterol: 0 mg, Fiber: 4 g

## Apple Chips

**Prep time:20 minutes| Cook time:2 hours| Serves 4**

- 1 teaspoon of ground cinnamon
- large apples, such as Honey crisp, Fuji, or Gala

1. Preheat the oven to 200 degrees Fahrenheit. Use a silicone baking mat or parchment paper to line two large baking sheets.
2. Using a mandolin, finely slice the apples to approximately 1/8-inch thick. Each slice should have the seeds removed. On the baking sheets, arrange the apple slices in a single layer. Cinnamon should be sprinkled on both sides, and bake the apples for one hour—Bake for another hour after flipping the apples. Please turn off the oven and allow the apples to cool for approximately 30 minutes before removing them. Continue baking the apples for 15 minutes if they are not crispy.
3. Take the apples off the baking pan, eat them right away, or keep them in the airtight container.

**PER SERVING**

Calories: 88 kcal, Protein: 1 g, Carbohydrates: 24 g, Fat: 1 g, Cholesterol: 0 mg, Fiber: 2.7 g

## Pita Chips

**Prep time:10 minutes| Cook time:10 minutes | Serves 4**

- 1/4 tsp of garlic powder
- 1 Tbsp. of grated Parmesan cheese
- 1/2 tsp of salt
- Cooking spray
- 1 Tbsp. of dried Italian seasoning
- (6-inch) pita bread (whole wheat)

1. Preheat the oven to 350 degrees Fahrenheit. Combine Parmesan, garlic powder, Italian seasoning, and salt in a mixing bowl. Each pita should be cut into eight wedges and then separated into two pieces.
2. Place on a baking sheet lined with parchment paper, and I was using a frying spray to coat the wedges. Season with the seasoning mix and bake for 10 minutes or golden brown. Allow cooling on the rack.

**PER SERVING**

Calories: 120 kcal, Protein: 4 g, Carbohydrates: 20 g, Fat: 3 g, Cholesterol: 2 mg, Fiber: 9 g

## Spicy Almonds

**Prep time: 10 minutes | Cook time: 20 minutes | Serves 6**

- 1 ½ cups almonds
- ½ tsp cayenne
- ¼ tsp onion powder
- ½ tsp garlic powder
- ½ tsp cumin powder
- 1 tsp paprika
- 1 ½ tsp Worcestershire sauce
- Salt

1. Preheat the oven to 350 F/ 180 C.
2. In a mixing bowl, mix almonds, Worcestershire sauce, paprika, cumin powder, garlic powder, onion powder, cayenne, and salt until well coated.
3. Spread almonds onto a parchment-lined baking sheet and bake in preheated oven for 15-20 minutes.
4. Serve and enjoy.

**PER SERVING**

Calories 142 ;Fat 12 g ;Carbohydrates 6 g ;Sugar 1.4 g ;Protein 5.2 g ;Cholesterol 0 mg

## Crispy Carrot Fries

**Prep time: 10 minutes | Cook time: 20 minutes | Serves 4**

- 3 large carrots, peel & cut into fries shape
- ½ tsp paprika
- ½ tsp onion powder
- 2 tbsp olive oil
- ¼ tsp chili powder
- 1 tsp garlic powder
- Pepper
- Salt

1. Preheat your air fryer to 350 F/ 180 C.
2. Tossing carrot fries with remaining ingredients in a mixing bowl until well coated.
3. Add carrot fries into the air fryer basket and cook for 15-20 minutes. Stir halfway through.
4. Serve and enjoy.

**PER SERVING**

Calories 87 ;Fat 7.1 g ;Carbohydrates 6.3 g ;Sugar 3 g ;Protein 0.7 g ;Cholesterol 0 mg

## Nutritious Roasted Chickpeas

**Prep time: 10 minutes | Cook time: 14 minutes | Serves 2**

- 14 oz can chickpeas, drained & rinsed
- 1 tsp dried oregano
- 1 tsp dried thyme
- 1 tsp dried rosemary
- 2 tbsp sesame oil
- 1 ½ tsp onion powder
- Pepper
- Salt

1. In a mixing bowl, toss chickpeas with oil, onion powder, rosemary, thyme, oregano, pepper, and salt until well coated.
2. Transfer chickpeas into the air fryer basket and cook at 370 F for 14 minutes. Stir halfway through.
3. Serve and enjoy.

**PER SERVING**

Calories 369 ;Fat 16.5 g ;Carbohydrates 47.6 g ;Sugar 0.6 g ;Protein 10.3 g ;Cholesterol 0 mg

## Curried Cannellini Bean Dip

**Prep time: 10 minutes | Cook time: 5 minutes | Serves 4**

- 14 oz can cannellini beans, drained & rinsed
- 1 tbsp fresh lemon juice
- 3 tbsp water
- ½ tsp curry powder
- 2 garlic cloves
- 2 tbsp Sriracha sauce
- 1½ tsp tamari sauce
- Salt

1. Add cannellini beans and remaining ingredients into the blender and blend until smooth and creamy.
2. Serve and enjoy.

**PER SERVING**

Calories 396 ;Fat 7.9 g ;Carbohydrates 60.6 g ;Sugar 2.4 g ;Protein 23.7 g ;Cholesterol 0 mg

## Cannellini Bean Hummus

**Prep time: 10 minutes | Cook time: 5 minutes | Serves 16**

- 30 oz can cannellini beans, drained & rinsed
- ¼ cup olive oil
- 1/8 tsp chili powder
- 1 tsp garlic powder
- 1 tsp cumin powder
- 3 tbsp fresh lemon juice
- ¼ cup water
- Salt

1. Add beans and remaining ingredients into the food processor and process until desired consistency.
2. Serve and enjoy.

**PER SERVING**

Calories 68 ;Fat 3.2 g ;Carbohydrates 9 g ;Sugar 0.2 g ;Protein 3.1 g ;Cholesterol 0 mg

## Black Bean Dip

**Prep time: 10 minutes | Cook time: 5 minutes | Serves 6**

- 14 oz can black beans, drained & rinsed
- ½ tsp cumin powder
- ¼ cup fresh lemon juice
- ¼ cup sesame oil
- ¼ cup tahini
- 4 garlic cloves
- Salt

1. Add black beans and remaining ingredients into the blender and blend until desired consistency.
2. Serve and enjoy.

**PER SERVING**

Calories 197 ;Fat 14.1 g ;Carbohydrates 14.7 g ;Sugar 0.6 g ;Protein 5.4 g ;Cholesterol 0 mg

## Healthy Beet Dip

**Prep time: 10 minutes | Cook time: 5 minutes | Serves 6**

- 2 large beets, roasted, peeled& chopped
- ½ cup sesame oil
- ¼ cup fresh lemon juice
- 1½ tbsp tahini
- 2 garlic cloves
- 2 tbsp almond flour
- 1 tsp cumin powder
- 1¼ cups walnuts
- Salt

1. Add chopped beets and remaining ingredients into the blender and blend until desired consistency.
2. Serve and enjoy.

**PER SERVING**

Calories 357 ;Fat 35.4 g ;Carbohydrates 7.3 g ;Sugar 2.6 g ;Protein 8 g ;Cholesterol 0 mg

## Easy Lentil Dip

**Prep time: 10 minutes | Cook time: 5 minutes | Serves 4**

- 1 cup cooked lentils
- 1 tsp onion powder
- 2 tbsp vegetable broth
- 2 tbsp peanut butter
- 3 garlic cloves
- 2 tbsp lemon basil vinegar
- 4 tbsp walnuts

1. Add cooked lentils and remaining ingredients into the blender and blend until desired consistency.
2. Serve and enjoy.

**PER SERVING**

Calories 285 ;Fat 9.7 g ;Carbohydrates 33.8 g ;Sugar 3 g ;Protein 16.9 g ;Cholesterol 0 mg

## Winter Perfect Guacamole

**Prep time: 10 minutes | Cook time: 5 minutes | Serves 8**

- 3 avocados, peel, pitted & chopped
- 1 jalapeno pepper, seeded & minced
- 1 tsp garlic, chopped
- 1½ tbsp fresh lemon juice
- 2 tbsp fresh parsley, chopped
- 1 large pear, core & chopped
- Pepper
- Salt

1. In a mixing bowl, mix chopped avocado and the remaining ingredients.
2. Serve and enjoy.

**PER SERVING**

Calories 166 ;Fat 14.8 g ;Carbohydrates 9.4 g ;Sugar 2.2 g ;Protein 1.6 g ;Cholesterol 0 mg.

# Chapter 14
## Desserts

## Lemon Cheesecake

**Prep time: 10 minutes | Cook time: 20 minutes |Serves 8**

- 1 envelope of unflavored gelatin
- 2 tablespoons of cold water
- 1/2 cup of skim milk; heat to boiling point
- 2 tablespoons of lemon juice
- Egg substitute equal to one egg or two egg whites
- 1 teaspoon of vanilla
- 1/4 cup of sugar
- lemon zest
- 2 cups of low-fat cottage cheese

1. Combine the gelatin, water, and lemon juice in a blender container. The process is for 1 to 2 minutes at low speed to soften gelatin.
2. Add the boiling milk and process until the gelatin is completely dissolved. Add egg replacement, vanilla, sugar, and cheese in a blender container, and blend until smooth.
3. Fill a 9-inch pie pan or a circular flat dish halfway with the mixture. Refrigerate for 2 to 3 hours. Just before serving, sprinkle with lemon zest if desired.

**PER SERVING**

Calories: 80 kcal, Protein: 9 g, Carbohydrates: 9 g, Fat: 1 g, Cholesterol: 3 mg, Fiber: 0.2 g

## Whole-Grain Mixed Berry Coffeecake

**Prep time: 10 minutes | Cook time: 30 minutes |Serves 8**

- 1 tablespoon of vinegar
- 1/2 cup of skim milk
- 1 teaspoon of vanilla
- 2 tablespoons of canola oil
- 1/3 cup of packed brown sugar
- 1 cup of pastry flour; whole-wheat
- 1/2 teaspoon of baking soda
- 1/8 teaspoon of salt
- 1/4 cup of low-fat slightly crushed granola,
- 1 cup of frozen mixed berries, such as raspberries, blueberries, and blackberries

1. Preheat the oven to 350 degrees Fahrenheit. Use a cooking spray to coat a cake pan or 8-inch round and coat it with flour.
2. Combine the vinegar, milk, oil, egg, vanilla, and brown sugar in a large mixing bowl and whisk until smooth. Just until moistened, stir in flour, cinnamon, baking soda, and salt. Fold half of the berries into the batter gently. Pour into the pan that has been prepared. Lastly, top with the granola and remaining berries.
3. Bake for 25 to 30 minutes, or until golden brown and the center of the top snaps back when touched. Cool for 10 minutes in the pan on a cooling rack. Warm the dish before serving.

**PER SERVING**

Calories: 165 kcal, Protein: 4 g, Carbohydrates: 26 g, Fat: 5 g, Cholesterol: 24 mg, Fiber: 3 g

## Almond and Apricot Biscotti

**Prep time: 20 minutes | Cook time: 60 minutes |Serves 24**

- 1/4 cup of brown sugar; firmly packed
- 2 lightly beaten eggs,
- 1 teaspoon of baking powder
- 3/4 cup of all-purpose flour (plain)
- 2 tablespoons of low-fat 1 percent milk
- 1/2 teaspoon of almond extract
- 2 tablespoons of canola oil
- 1/4 cup of coarsely chopped almonds.
- 2 tablespoons of dark honey
- 3/4 cup of whole-wheat flour; (whole-meal)
- 2/3 cup of dried apricots; chopped.

1. Preheat an oven to 350 degrees Fahrenheit. Combine the brown sugar, flours, and baking powder in a large mixing bowl. To combine ingredients, whisk them together. Add the milk, eggs, honey, canola oil, and almond extract to a mixing bowl. Stir the dough with the wooden spoon until it barely comes together. Add chopped apricots and almonds. Mix until the dough is well-blended using floured hands.
2. Shape the dough into a flattened log 3 inches wide, 12 inches long, and approximately 1-inch-high on a long piece of plastic and wrap by hand. Transfer the dough to a nonstick baking sheet by lifting the plastic wrap. Bake for 25 to 30 minutes, or until gently browned. Allow it cool for 10 minutes on another baking sheet.
3. On a cutting board, place the cooled log. Cut 24 1/2-inch broad slices diagonally crosswise using a serrated knife. Arrange the slices on the baking sheet, cut-side down. Put it back in the oven and bake for 15 to 20 minutes, or until crisp. Allow cooling fully before transferring to a wire rack. Keep the container sealed.

**PER SERVING**

Calories: 75 kcal, Protein: 2 g, Carbohydrates: 12 g, Fat: 2 g, Cholesterol: 15 mg, Fiber: 1 g

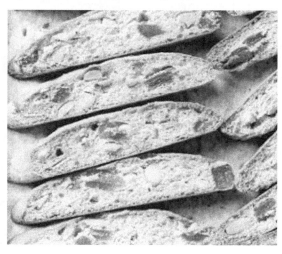

## Apple Dumplings

**Prep time: 2 hours | Cook time: 30 minutes |Serves 8**

### DOUGH:

- 2 tablespoons of apple liquor or brandy
- 1 tablespoon of butter
- 2 tablespoons of buckwheat flour
- 1 teaspoon of honey
- 2 tablespoons of rolled oats.
- 1 cup of whole-wheat flour

### APPLE FILLING:

- 1 teaspoon of nutmeg
- 6 large thinly sliced tart apples,
- Zest of 1 lemon
- 2 tablespoons of honey

1. Preheat an oven to 350 degrees Fahrenheit. Combine the flours, honey, butter, and oats in a food processor. Pulse a few times more until the mixture resembles a fine meal.
2. Pulse a few more times to incorporate the brandy or apple liquor until the mixture begins to form a ball. Refrigerate it for two hours after removing the mixture from the food processor. Combine nutmeg, apples, and honey. Toss in the lemon zest. Set it aside.
3. Extra flour is used to roll out the chilled dough to a thickness of 1/4 inch. Using an 8-inch circle cutter, cut the dough into 8-inch circles.
4. Use an 8-cup muffin pan that has been gently sprayed with cooking spray. Place a dough circle over each gently sprayed cup. Gently press dough into place. Fill them with the apple mixture. To seal, fold over the edges, squeeze the top, and bake for 30 minutes or golden brown.

### PER SERVING

Calories: 178 kcal, Protein: 3 g, Carbohydrates: 36 g, Fat: 2.5 g, Cholesterol: 4 mg, Fiber: 1 g

## Carrot and Spice Quick Bread

**Prep time: 15 minutes | Cook time: 45 minutes |Serves 17**

- 1 cup of whole-wheat flour
- 1 teaspoon of grated orange rind
- 1/2 cup of all-purpose flour; sifted.
- 1 tablespoon of walnuts; finely chopped.
- 1/4 cup and 2 tablespoons of brown sugar; firmly packed
- 1/2 teaspoon of ground cinnamon
- 1 1/2 cups of shredded carrots
- 1/4 teaspoon of ground ginger
- ½ tablespoons of golden raisins
- 1/2 teaspoon of baking soda
- 1/3 cup of skim milk
- 1 beaten egg whites/ egg substitute equal to 1 egg,
- 1 teaspoon of vanilla extract
- ¾ tablespoons of unsweetened orange juice
- 1/3 cup of margarine; trans-fat-free, softened.
- ½ teaspoons of baking powder

1. Preheat the oven to 375 degrees Fahrenheit. Cooking spray coats a 2 ½ by 4 ½ by 8 ½ inch loaf pan.
2. Combine the dry flours, baking soda, powder, cinnamon, and ginger in a small dish and set them aside.
3. In a large mixing bowl, blend margarine and sugar using an electric mixer or by hand. Add orange juice, milk, vanilla, egg, and orange rind in a mixing bowl. Stir in raisins, carrots, and walnuts in a mixing bowl. Add dry ingredients that have been set aside. Mix thoroughly.
4. Preheat the oven to 350°F and bake for about 45 mins, or until a wooden pick inserted in the middle comes out clean. Pour the batter into the loaf pan. Allow 10 minutes to cool in the pan. Remove the pan from the oven and cool fully on a wire rack.

### PER SERVING

Calories: 110 kcal, Protein: 2 g, Carbohydrates: 15 g, Fat: 5 g, Cholesterol: traces, Fiber: 1 g

## Grapes And Lemon Sour Cream Sauce

**Prep time: 10 minutes | Cook time: 0 minutes |Serves 6**

- 2 tablespoons of powdered sugar
- 1/2 cup of sour cream; fat-free
- 1/2 teaspoon of lemon zest
- 1/8 teaspoon of vanilla extract
- 1/2 teaspoon of lemon juice
- 1 1/2 cups of seedless red grapes
- 3 tablespoons of chopped walnuts
- 1 1/2 cups of seedless green grapes

1. Combine lemon juice, powdered sugar, sour cream, lemon zest, and vanilla in a small mixing bowl. To ensure an equal distribution of ingredients, whisk them together. Refrigerate for several hours after covering.
2. In six stemmed dessert cups or bowls, place equal parts of grapes, top each dish with a dollop of sauce and 1/2 spoonful of chopped walnuts. Serve right away.

### PER SERVING

Calories: 106 kcal, Protein: 2 g, Carbohydrates: 208 g, Fat: 2 g, Cholesterol: 2 mg, Fiber: 1 g

## Orange Dream Smoothie

**Prep time: 10 minutes | Cook time: 0 minutes |Serves 4**

- 1 1/2 cups of chilled orange juice
- 1 teaspoon of grated orange zest
- 1 cup of soy milk; light vanilla, chilled
- 1/3 cup of soft or silken tofu
- 1 tablespoon of dark honey
- 1/2 teaspoon of vanilla extract
- 4 peeled orange segments
- 5 ice cubes

1. Blend the blender with soy milk, orange juice, vanilla, tofu, orange zest, honey, and ice cubes. Blend for approximately 30 seconds or until smooth and foamy.
2. Pour into long chilled glasses, and with an orange segment, garnish each glass.

**PER SERVING**

Calories: 101 kcal, Protein: 3 g, Carbohydrates: 20 g, Fat: 1 g, Cholesterol: 0 mg, Fiber: 1 g

## Rustic Apple-Cranberry Tart

**Prep time: 10 minutes | Cook time: 50 minutes |Serves 8**

**FOR THE FILLING:**

- 1/4 cup of apple juice
- 1/2 cup of dried cranberries
- 1/4 teaspoon of ground cinnamon
- 2 tablespoons of corn starch
- 1 teaspoon of vanilla extract
- 4 large cored, peeled, sliced tart apples,

**FOR THE CRUST:**

- 2 teaspoons of sugar
- 1 1/4 cups of whole-wheat flour (whole-meal)
- 1/4 cup of ice water
- 3 tablespoons of trans-free margarine

1. Combine the apple juice and cranberries in a small microwave-safe bowl. Cook for 1 minute on high, then stir. Cover and leave aside for 1 hour, or until mixture is near to room temperature. Continue to cook the apple juice for 30 sec at a time, tossing after each interval, until it is extremely warm.
2. Preheat an oven to 375 degrees Fahrenheit. Combine the apple slices and cornstarch in a large mixing bowl. Toss well to get an equal coating. Add juice and cranberries to a mixing bowl. Mix thoroughly. Add cinnamon and vanilla to a mixing bowl. Put it aside.
3. In a large mixing bowl, combine flour and sugar to make the crust. Add sliced margarine into the mixture and mix well until crumbly. Add one tablespoon of ice water and stir with a fork until the dough forms a rough lump.
4. Place a big sheet of aluminum foil on the surface and tape it down. It should be dusted with flour. Flatten the dough in the middle of the foil. Roll the dough from the center to the edges with a

rolling pin to form a 13-inch-diameter circle. Add fruit filling in the dough's middle. Cover the dough with the filling, leaving about a 1- to 2-inch border. Fold the crust's top and bottom edges up over the filling. The pastry will not completely cover the contents; it should have a rustic appearance.

5. Remove the foil and the countertop from the tape. Cover the tart with another piece of foil to cover the exposed fruit. Slide the tart onto a baking sheet, top and bottom foil included, and bake for 30 minutes. Remove the foil from the top and bake for another 10 minutes or browned. Serve immediately after cutting into 8 wedges.

**PER SERVING**

Calories: 197 kcal, Protein: 3 g, Carbohydrates: 35 g, Fat: 5 g, Cholesterol: 0 mg, Fiber: 5 g

## Strawberries And Cream

**Prep time: 10 minutes | Cook time: 0 minutes |Serves 6**

- 1/2 cup of brown sugar
- 1 1/2 cups of sour cream; fat-free
- 1 quart fresh hulled and halved strawberries; (6 whole for garnish)
- 2 tablespoons of amaretto liqueur

1. Whisk the brown sugar, sour cream, and liqueur in a small bowl.
2. Combine the sour cream mixture and halved strawberries in a large mixing bowl. To combine, carefully stir everything together. Cover and chill for 1 hour or until well cooked.
3. Fill 6 chilled sherbet glasses or colored bowls halfway with strawberries. Serve immediately with whole strawberries as a garnish.

**PER SERVING**

Calories: 136 kcal, Protein: 3 g, Carbohydrates: 31 g, Fat: traces, Cholesterol: 6 mg, Fiber: 5 g

## Delicious & Healthy Rice Pudding

**Prep time: 10 minutes | Cook time: 15 minutes | Serves 4**

- 4 cups cooked black rice
- 1 tbsp vanilla
- 3 dates, pitted & chopped
- ½ cup frozen blueberries
- ½ cup frozen raspberries
- 1 cup frozen strawberries
- ¾ cup dried cherries, diced
- 4 cups unsweetened coconut milk

1. Add cooked rice and remaining ingredients into the saucepan and bring to a boil.
2. Turn heat to low and simmer for 15 minutes.
3. Stir well and serve.

**PER SERVING**

Calories 840 ;Fat 58.4 g ;Carbohydrates 75.3 g ;Sugar 24.2 g ;Protein 13.1 g ;Cholesterol 2 mg

## Baked Apple Slices

**Prep time: 10 minutes | Cook time: 30 minutes | Serves 4**

- 4 medium apples, core & slice
- ¼ tsp ground cinnamon
- ¼ tsp ground nutmeg
- 1 tbsp coconut oil, melted

1. Preheat the oven to 375 F.
2. Add apple slices into the baking dish, drizzle with coconut oil, and sprinkle with cinnamon and nutmeg.
3. Bake for 25-30 minutes.
4. Serve and enjoy.

**PER SERVING**

Calories 146 ;Fat 3.9 g ;Carbohydrates 31 g ;Sugar 23.2 g ;Protein 0.6 g ;Cholesterol 0 mg

## Baked Figs

**Prep time: 5 minutes | Cook time: 15 minutes | Serves 8**

- 8 figs, quarters
- ¼ cup maple syrup

1. Preheat the oven to 350 F/ 180 C.
2. Arrange figs onto a parchment-lined baking sheet, drizzle with maple syrup, and bake in a preheated oven for 10-15 minutes.
3. Serve and enjoy.

**PER SERVING**

Calories 80 ;Fat 0.2 g ;Carbohydrates 20.9 g ;Sugar 17.8 g ;Protein 0.7 g ;Cholesterol 0 mg

## Healthy Quinoa Pudding

**Prep time: 10 minutes | Cook time: 18 minutes | Serves 2**

- 2/3 cup quinoa, rinsed
- ¼ tsp cinnamon
- 2 tbsp agave syrup
- 1 tsp vanilla
- 1 cup unsweetened soy milk
- Pinch of salt

1. Add quinoa, milk, and remaining ingredients into the saucepan and cook over medium heat until pudding is thickened and quinoa is cooked.
2. Stir well and serve.

**PER SERVING**

Calories 288 ;Fat 5.2 g ;Carbohydrates 51.3 g ;Sugar 12.2 g ;Protein 8.5 g ;Cholesterol 0 mg

## Chocolate Yogurt

**Prep time: 5 minutes | Cook time: 5 minutes | Serves 1**

- 1 cup Greek yogurt
- 1 tbsp unsweetened soy milk
- 1 tsp maple syrup
- 2 tbsp unsweetened cocoa powder

1. Add all ingredients into the blender and blend until smooth.
2. Pour blended mixture into the air-tight container, cover, and place in the freezer for 3 hours.
3. Serve chilled and enjoy.

**PER SERVING**

Calories 200 ;Fat 5.7 g ;Carbohydrates 19.8 g ;Sugar 14 g ;Protein 22.4 g ;Cholesterol 10 mg

## Healthy Summer Yogurt

**Prep time: 10 minutes | Cook time: 5 minutes | Serves 6**

- 2 cups frozen berries
- 1 tsp vanilla
- ½ cup Greek yogurt
- 2 tbsp maple syrup
- 2 frozen bananas

1. Add all ingredients into the blender and blend until smooth.
2. Pour blended mixture into the air-tight container, cover, and place in the freezer for 3 hours.
3. Serve chilled and enjoy.

**PER SERVING**

Calories 99 ;Fat 1.2 g ;Carbohydrates 18.9 g ;Sugar 14.8 g ;Protein 3 g ;Cholesterol 4 mg

## Mango Popsicles

**Prep time: 10 minutes | Cook time: 5 minutes | Serves 6**

- 2 mangoes, peeled & diced
- 2 tbsp maple syrup
- 1 lime juice
- 14 oz can coconut milk

1. Add mangoes, maple syrup, lime juice, and coconut milk into the blender and blend until smooth.
2. Pour mango mixture into the popsicle molds and place in the refrigerator until set.
3. Serve chilled and enjoy.

**PER SERVING**

Calories 221 ;Fat 14.6 g ;Carbohydrates 24.6 g ;Sugar 21.2 g ;Protein 2.3 g ;Cholesterol 0 mg

# Appendix 1 Measurement Conversion Chart

| Volume Equivalents (Dry) | |
|---|---|
| US STANDARD | METRIC (APPROXIMATE) |
| 1/8 teaspoon | 0.5 mL |
| 1/4 teaspoon | 1 mL |
| 1/2 teaspoon | 2 mL |
| 3/4 teaspoon | 4 mL |
| 1 teaspoon | 5 mL |
| 1 tablespoon | 15 mL |
| 1/4 cup | 59 mL |
| 1/2 cup | 118 mL |
| 3/4 cup | 177 mL |
| 1 cup | 235 mL |
| 2 cups | 475 mL |
| 3 cups | 700 mL |
| 4 cups | 1 L |

| Weight Equivalents | |
|---|---|
| US STANDARD | METRIC (APPROXIMATE) |
| 1 ounce | 28 g |
| 2 ounces | 57 g |
| 5 ounces | 142 g |
| 10 ounces | 284 g |
| 15 ounces | 425 g |
| 16 ounces (1 pound) | 455 g |
| 1.5 pounds | 680 g |
| 2 pounds | 907 g |

| Volume Equivalents (Liquid) | | |
|---|---|---|
| US STANDARD | US STANDARD (OUNCES) | METRIC (APPROXIMATE) |
| 2 tablespoons | 1 fl.oz. | 30 mL |
| 1/4 cup | 2 fl.oz. | 60 mL |
| 1/2 cup | 4 fl.oz. | 120 mL |
| 1 cup | 8 fl.oz. | 240 mL |
| 1 1/2 cup | 12 fl.oz. | 355 mL |
| 2 cups or 1 pint | 16 fl.oz. | 475 mL |
| 4 cups or 1 quart | 32 fl.oz. | 1 L |
| 1 gallon | 128 fl.oz. | 4 L |

| Temperatures Equivalents | |
|---|---|
| FAHRENHEIT(F) | CELSIUS(C) APPROXIMATE |
| 225 °F | 107 °C |
| 250 °F | 120 ° °C |
| 275 °F | 135 °C |
| 300 °F | 150 °C |
| 325 °F | 160 °C |
| 350 °F | 180 °C |
| 375 °F | 190 °C |
| 400 °F | 205 °C |
| 425 °F | 220 °C |
| 450 °F | 235 °C |
| 475 °F | 245 °C |
| 500 °F | 260 °C |

# Appendix 2 The Dirty Dozen and Clean Fifteen

The Environmental Working Group (EWG) is a nonprofit, nonpartisan organization dedicated to protecting human health and the environment Its mission is to empower people to live healthier lives in a healthier environment. This organization publishes an annual list of the twelve kinds of produce, in sequence, that have the highest amount of pesticide residue-the Dirty Dozen-as well as a list of the fifteen kinds ofproduce that have the least amount of pesticide residue-the Clean Fifteen.

| THE DIRTY DOZEN | |
| --- | --- |
| The 2016 Dirty Dozen includes the following produce. These are considered among the year's most important produce to buy organic: | |
| Strawberries | Spinach |
| Apples | Tomatoes |
| Nectarines | Bell peppers |
| Peaches | Cherry tomatoes |
| Celery | Cucumbers |
| Grapes | Kale/collard greens |
| Cherries | Hot peppers |

The Dirty Dozen list contains two additional itemskale/collard greens and hot peppers-because they tend to contain trace levels of highly hazardous pesticides.

| THE CLEAN FIFTEEN | |
| --- | --- |
| The least critical to buy organically are the Clean Fifteen list. The following are on the 2016 list: | |
| Avocados | Papayas |
| Corn | Kiw |
| Pineapples | Eggplant |
| Cabbage | Honeydew |
| Sweet peas | Grapefruit |
| Onions | Cantaloupe |
| Asparagus | Cauliflower |
| Mangos | |

Some of the sweet corn sold in the United States are made from genetically engineered (GE) seedstock. Buy organic varieties of these crops to avoid GE produce.

# Appendix 3 Index

**LINDA J. PEREZ**